A Walking Tour
Ahmedabad

A Walking Tour
Ahmedabad

Sketches of the City's Architectural Treasures

Matthijs van Oostrum and Gregory Bracken

MAPIN PUBLISHING

We are grateful to adani˙ for their generous support towards the publication of this book.

First published in India in 2017
Mapin Publishing
706 Kaivanna, Panchvati, Ellisbridge,
Ahmedabad 380006 INDIA

Simultaneously published in the
United States of America in 2017 by
Grantha Corporation
77 Daniele Drive, Hidden Meadows,
Ocean Township, NJ 07712
E: mapin@mapinpub.com

Distributors
North America
Antique Collectors' Club
T: +1 800 252 5231 • F: +413 529 0862
E: sales@antiquecc.com
www.accdistribution.com/us

United Kingdom and Europe
Gazelle Book Services Ltd.
T: +44 1524 528 500 • F: +44 1524 528 510
E: sales@gazellebooks.co.uk
www.gazellebookservices.co.uk

Thailand, Laos, Cambodia and Myanmar
Paragon Asia Co. Ltd
T: +66 2877 7755 • F: +66 2468 9636
E: info@paragonasia.com

Malaysia
Areca Books
T: +604 2610307
E: arecabooks@gmail.com

Rest of the World
Mapin Publishing Pvt. Ltd
T: +91 79 40 228 228 • F: +91 79 40 228 201
E: mapin@mapinpub.com
www.mapinpub.com

Text © Matthijs van Oostrum
Illustrations © Gregory Bracken

ISBN: 978-93-85360-17-6 (Mapin)
ISBN: 978-1-935677-74-1 (Grantha)
LCCN: 2016951191

Copyediting: Ankona Das / Mapin Editorial
Editorial Supervision & Proofreading: Neha Manke / Mapin Editorial
Design: Gopal Limbad / Mapin Design Studio
Production: Mapin Design Studio
Printed at Parksons Graphics, Mumbai

CONTENTS

Introduction

Ahmedabad is a city with a tremendously rich architectural history. Coming to a full appreciation of the city's treasures will surely be a worthwhile endeavour and should also contain some delightful surprises. In a country full of significant ancient monuments and booming new cities what sets Ahmedabad apart is that it shares the heritage of a great medieval past with important pre-modern and contemporary buildings as well. Although inhabited since the eleventh century, the city dates its foundation to the early fifteenth century and has almost always prospered, with significant buildings being constructed throughout every historical period. The most distinctive part of Ahmedabad is its old walled city with its *pol*s and *haveli*s, and no city in India contains such a large and well-preserved medieval city where long-lost urban forms and architecture can still be seen.

This architectural guidebook aims to provide the reader with detailed information on more than 140 buildings arranged across 11 walks. Each chapter shows a suggested route, and each follows on from where the previous one left off. Each walk covers a particular area in the city, like Bhadra or Shahibaug. The book has been written to appeal to anyone interested in learning about Ahmedabad's rich architectural heritage, one that stretches back over 600 years that can be divided into roughly four stages and buildings from all these periods have been included in this guidebook. The city was founded by Ahmed Shah in 1411 and his dynasty ruled it for 150 years. Subsequently conquered by the Mughals, then by Marathas, both of these groups added their own distinctive styles to the city's architectural legacy. The third historical period was British colonial rule, which started in 1818 and lasted for more than a century. Finally, after Independence in 1947, a range of architects, both foreign and local have greatly added to Ahmedabad's heritage.

From its very inception, Ahmedabad has always provided room for a wide range of communities. This mix is reflected in its architecture as building styles, materials and even the symbolism of the different communities are moulded together to form a quintessential Ahmedabadi (or Amdavadi) style.

Ahmedabad is also a mercantile city, always looking for a way to make a handsome profit. The merchants and industrialists of the past used their wealth to provide patronage to the many temples and institutions dotted around the city. They also invited internationally renowned architects to build many of them. It is our sincere hope that this book will be useful to anyone with an interest in architecture, and better help them appreciate the architectural gem that is Ahmedabad.

History of Ahmedabad

The area that now houses the city of Ahmedabad was inhabited for a number of centuries before its official foundation. In the area of what is now occupied by the Jamalpur and Mirzapur neighbourhoods an earlier town existed, called **Ashawal**. This town is mentioned in several historic and religious sources and they tell us that Ashawal had a sizeable Jain community and was well connected to local trade networks. The region of Gujarat was at this time ruled by the Solanki dynasty, followers of the Hindu religion. In 1297 it was conquered by the Sultan of Delhi, of the Khilji dynasty, who first introduced Islam into the region. The Delhi sultans remained in control of the area for close to a century until internal struggles between two rival members of the Tughluq dynasty erupted in the 1390s. Into this weakened state of affairs came crashing the invasion of the Mongol army of Timur (Tamerlane) in 1398, which effectively ended consolidated rule and various parts of the Delhi Sultanate broke away to form independent states. The Gujarat Sultanate was founded in 1407 by Zafar Khan, but it was still without a capital city. In 1411, the city of **Ahmedabad was founded** by Sultan Ahmed Shah, son of Zafar Khan. The site for the capital had a central position in the kingdom his father had carved out. Furthermore, one of his religious mentors, Ganj Baksh, had already settled in the region and there were existing trading networks which would prove essential to the success of the city.

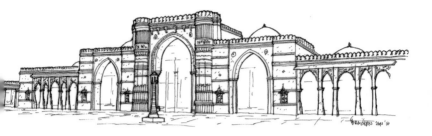

Ahmed Shah laid out the city according to Persian planning principles. All of the main elements of the early city were arranged along an east-west axis perpendicular to the Sabarmati River. Ahmed Shah's fortified residence stood on the western limit of the axis. The fort looked out over the *maidan*, a large open ground for ceremonial functions that extended towards Teen Darwaza. Beyond Teen Darwaza was the market area that terminated at the Friday Mosque or Jama Masjid, which was the religious centre of the city. As already noted, the area already had existing Jain and Hindu residents, but to attract more people, noblemen were invited to settle at the Sultan's court. The residences of these noblemen became the nuclei of new neighbourhoods or *pur*s that still characterize the city (Mirzapur, Kalupur, etc.). Under the Sultanate rule Ahmedabad grew rapidly and prospered, especially under the long reign of **Sultan Mahmud Begada** (1458 to 1511), which greatly enhanced the city, with many historic monuments that have survived from that time to this date. Sultan Mahmud Begada expanded the borders of the Gujarat Sultanate by military conquest and decided to build a new capital at Champaner. Despite this, the growth of Ahmedabad continued and improvements were made to the city's defences. Mahmud Begada commissioned the construction of city walls, the size of which shows the rapid expansion of the city at that time. Ahmedabad's Muslim rulers stimulated trade and offered patronage to Sufi religious scholars, and both the complexes of Sarkhej and Shah-e-Alam, outside the city walls date from this time.

The wealth of India's cities, including places like Ahmedabad, lured European traders. Vasco da Gama was the first to find a direct sea

Timeline

Ashawal ▶	10th c.
	1297 ⟨ Gujarat conquered by Delhi Sultanate
City founded by Ahmed Shah I ▶	1411
	1458 ⟨ Reign of Mahmud Begada begins
Conquest of Malwa region and the foundation of Champaner ▶	1484
	1487 ⟨ Construction of city walls
Battle of Diu (in which the Sultanate was defeated by the Portuguese) ▶	1537
	1573 ⟨ Sultanate annexed by the Mughal empire
Arrival of the British East India Company ▶	1613
	1628 ⟨ Shah Jahan becomes Mughal emperor
Nominal victory by the Maratha Empire ▶	1707
	1758 ⟨ Official incorporation into the Maratha Empire
British East India Company conquers Ahmedabad ▶	1780
	1818 ⟨ British East India Company rule
Rann of Kutch earthquake ▶	1819
	1861 ⟨ First textile mill founded (by Ranchhodlal Chhotalal)
Opening of train station ▶	1863
	1915 ⟨ Mahatma Gandhi arrives in Ahmedabad
Indian Independence ▶	1947
	1951 ⟨ Le Corbusier comes to India
Establishment of the state of Gujarat ▶	1960
	2001 ⟨ Bhuj earthquake

route to India from Europe, but he was only one of the myriad of traders already connecting the cities across the Indian Ocean. The mainstay of Ahmedabad's economy was the production of textiles. Gujarat has a climate well suited to the production of cotton, and the growing, spinning, weaving and dyeing of this material created mass employment as also fabulous wealth for some. Gujarat's coastline— the longest in India—was dotted with countless ports exporting goods but Ahmedabad's independence came to an end in 1573 when the armies of the **Mughal Empire**, superior in numbers and guns, conquered the city. Ahmedabad lost its role as a capital and became a province ruled by an appointed governor. As a consequence, this period saw very little construction because the tax collected went to embellish the imperial Mughal cities of Delhi and Agra.

Yet Mughal rule ensured peace, which greatly enhanced trade and manufacturing. By the seventeenth century Ahmedabad had become one of the 20 largest cities in the world and this attracted the attention of the European trading companies. The British East India Company had already established itself here in 1613, and was soon followed by the Dutch East India Company. The combination of the political stability of the Mughals and the increased market demand from European traders laid the foundations for the vast wealth for a class of merchants who would come to dominate the city's future. Towards the end of the seventeenth century Mughal strength under Aurangzeb's reign was decreasing and the competing **Maratha Empire** was gaining more and more territory, eventually defeating a Mughal army near Ahmedabad in 1707, but they agreed to retreat after substantial payments had been made. In 1758 they returned once again and invaded the city and the eighteenth century is seen as a period of instability and decline, both of urban growth and the city's wealth. Frequent raids, and changes in power, devastated the accumulated wealth of the city, yet, architecturally, this period is of key importance as the merchant class invested their money in the construction of the grand *haveli*s, houses arranged in winding *pol*s and protected by reinforced gates that kept the inhabitants safe from the looting and violence outside.

The **British East India Company** had been militarily expanding its trading empire for decades and in 1780 conquered Ahmedabad. In a repeat of the events of 73 years earlier, a pact was made and the Maratha Empire continued to rule for another 38 years, before the city was finally annexed by the British in 1818. A devastating earthquake the following year levelled many of the city's buildings, and although Ahmedabad was again being ruled by a foreign power, the city greatly profited from the political stability that the new administration offered, especially the many new institutions they set up. The British administrators found themselves in charge of a city that had been devastated and they made it their colonial mission to rebuild, educate the people, and promote the study of the sciences. This period saw the construction of many schools, libraries and hospitals. In 1858 the Municipal Government was established and started to improve the civic infrastructure in the city and in 1864 a railway line was opened to Bombay (now Mumbai). Many of these ventures were actively supported by the Ahmedabadi merchant class, who also often financed them, especially the Jain community which was powerful (many Jain temples date from this period).

Yet, all was not well. The Uprising of 1857 that swept across India showed that an increase in wealth and welfare had come about alongside a growing dissatisfaction that ordinary Indians were not in charge of their own country. The secluded *pol* houses that once protected the Ahmedabadis from raids and looting had now become the harbingers of a growing freedom movement. Adding to the discontent were the cheap English textiles that were destroying the native industry for which the city was famous. A key turning point was in 1861, when the first textile mill was founded in Ahmedabad. In subsequent years, 41 more mills were founded and Ahmedabad became known as the **Manchester of the East**.

These conditions were instrumental in **Mahatma Gandhi's** decision to settle on Ahmedabad as his base for India's struggle for independence in 1915. Gandhi stayed in Ahmedabad for 18 years and in that period he grew to become the Father of the Nation. He left Ahmedabad in 1933 for the great Salt March that proved to be a decisive turning point in the struggle for independence. It took another 14 years, and a World War, for the British to finally grant India its **Independence** in 1947. The newly gained independence gave Indians the confidence to reshape their country. Foreign architects like Le Corbusier and Louis Kahn were invited by politicians and members of the merchant class to come

Mahatma Gandhi in Ahmedabad

1915 Mahatma Gandhi arrives in Ahmedabad
Kocharab Ashram.. Walk 10 **Kocharab**

1917 Establishment of Gandhi Ashram
Gandhi Ashram ....Walk 7 **Shahibaug**

1920 Meeting to convince students of non-cooperation movement
Gujarat College... Walk 10 **Kocharab**

1922 Mahatma Gandhi tried for sedition
Circuit House ....Walk 7 **Shahibaug**

1925 After being released, Mahatma Gandhi opens his university
Gujarat Vidyapith .... Walk 8 **Ashram Road**

1930 Mahatma Gandhi departs on Salt March
Gandhi statue... Walk 8 **Ashram Road**

1933 Statue of Chinubhai Ranchhodlal unveiled by Mahatma Gandhi
Bhadra plaza.. Walk 1 **Bhadra area**

to the city. Building on their ideas of Modernity, a new generation of Indian architects tried to integrate this modern thought into the Indian context and climate. A whole range of educational institutes came into being that exemplified this architectural thought and put Ahmedabad on the international map yet again. Since Independence Ahmedabad has seen immense growth in population, from around 600,000 inhabitants in 1950 to more than 6 million today. Compared with other Indian megacities, Ahmedabad has been better able to keep up with this pace of growth, and provide ample land and infrastructure for development. Yet, during the second part of the twentieth century, many historic buildings were encroached upon due to a lack of proper maintenance funds. In recent years the municipal government has been keen to redevelop some of Ahmedabad's most historic places.

A Note on Climate

Ahmedabad has a hot semi-arid climate and in the summer months (between April and June) temperatures can rise to dizzying heights of more than 45°C (113°F). Although many historic buildings have been suitably adapted to deal with the climate, being outside at all during this period is unpleasant. The best time to see Ahmedabad is in the cooler winter months from November till February. Temperatures in winter are around 25°C (77°F), but can drop dramatically at night to as low as 7°C (45°F). Walking is most pleasant in the mornings as the midday sun has an intense presence all year round. Monsoon usually starts in early June, but the timing can vary by a number of weeks year on year. The monsoon rains are irregularly spread across the season for around 30 days. They bring some relief in temperature but also add to the humidity. Mosquitoes breed in pools of (stagnant) water and hatch from August to November. Nowadays, the main danger they pose is in the spread of the dengue fever (malaria is, thankfully, uncommon in urban areas). In a normal healthy person dengue fever can last for about a week and is usually not life threatening.

Nonetheless, if contracted, the fever will require immediate treatment in hospital. The best protection against mosquitoes is clothing that covers the body and the use of any number of anti-mosquito sprays and lotions which can be bought at supermarkets and pharmacies.

A Note on Local Customs

Ahmedabad is a city of many diverse traditions, religions and customs. In using this book please respect these traditions and be accommodating towards their requirements when visiting buildings. Here are listed

some general behavioural rules, but do note that exceptions may apply to specific places. All temples and mosques will require you to take off your shoes before entering. Some mosques also require you to cover your head. Mosques are closed during prayer time to non-Muslim visitors. Mosques and temples are generally open to the public and free of charge but might be closed for certain festivals or special occasions. The societal and religious mixture that created some of the most beautiful buildings in Ahmedabad has led, unfortunately, to periodical caste-based and religious tension, most notably in 2002 when clashes between Hindus and Muslims claimed a number of lives. It is important to note that these clashes are the exception and that the various communities co-exist peacefully on a day-to-day basis, and have done so for centuries.

This book also includes a number of private residences, with descriptions of their beautiful interiors. Even if eager to see some of these interiors, please understand that these houses remain private residences and that these buildings are not officially open to the public. Yet, the residents are proud of their living heritage and they might allow you to enter. If lucky enough to be invited inside, please ensure you remove your shoes before entering and respect the private property of the resident. Likewise, educational campuses and other institutional buildings may have restrictions on entering. The architecture here is not officially listed, so visiting may sometimes be frowned upon. The guards usually have authority to restrict entry, so make sure you explain your purpose for visiting; that it is the architecture you are interested in.

Photography is allowed on all public streets and lanes, unless otherwise indicated. Photography is also allowed inside most buildings (except museums) but do respect the rule to not to take photos if so required. Institutions especially seem to be suspicious of photography. Unless otherwise indicated, all buildings listed in this book are free of charge. Even most museums do not charge admission, but they do usually require you to sign a register before entering, as do some other public buildings.

A Note on Finding your Way
The architectural sites in this book have been arranged in 11 walks that guide you through the city. Every new walk starts where the previous one ended so that you can interlink them all. To find your way, every walk has been provided with a plan, and directions are given in the

text. Although most streets in Ahmedabad have official names, these are rarely used and people prefer to give directions using landmarks. Commonly used street names have been included. Ahmedabad has a very well-functioning Rapid Bus System (BRTS) with cheap fares and genuinely fast service. The BRTS, officially called Janmarg, started running in 2009 and has increased to 89 kilometres of bus routes. It has since won various awards and many new lines are being planned. There are also two metro lines currently under construction, which are planned to start operating in 2018. Rickshaws provide another great means of moving around quickly and Ahmedabad is probably the only city in India where the meters are actually used (which saves you time on haggling about the price). All drivers will have a conversion chart to calculate the fare (expect to pay roughly half of the number that the meter indicates). The traffic in Ahmedabad can have a somewhat disorganized character. Vehicles can come at you from any direction, and at speed. Traffic is organized around a clear hierarchy of vehicles with lots of honking of horns. Cows are holy and thus at the top of the hierarchy. Below these come buses, trucks, cars and rickshaws. As a pedestrian you are the lowest in this hierarchy, so do not expect anyone to stop for you. The lanes of the old city can sometimes get clogged with traffic, so one advantage of being a pedestrian is that you can overtake the rows of stationary vehicles. Despite improvements that have been achieved on limiting exhaust fumes; the air is still quite polluted, so avoid travelling during rush hour if possible.

CLASSIFIED ITINERARIES

Ahmedabad City Map

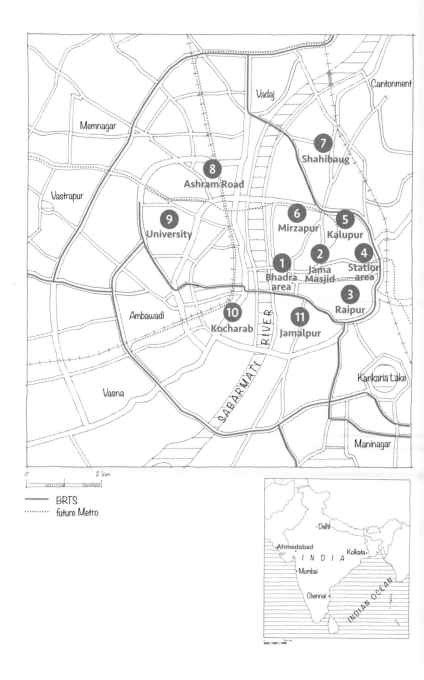

0   2 Km

——— BRTS
········· future Metro

WALKS

The Bhadra fort was the location of the fortified residence of the rulers of Ahmedabad for hundreds of years. It was here that Ahmed Shah first founded the city in 1411 AD and built his palace and private mosque that rank among the oldest surviving buildings of the city. Although now heavily encroached upon, most of the palace consisted of lush gardens that were fed by water from the Sabarmati River. In recent times, the walls of the fort, except on the riverfront side, have come down and space has opened up for modern buildings. Prominent people and institutes were able to settle in close proximity to the symbolic heart of the city. The area also has many street vendors, fuelled by the crowds of people coming in and out of the Lal Darwaza bus stand, which is the terminal station for most municipal bus services.

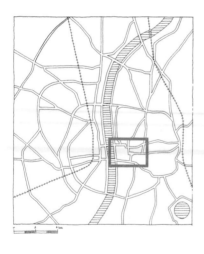

Key

1 Manek Burj

2 Ahmed Shah Masjid

3 Congress Bhavan

4 Irish Presbyterian Mission High School

5 Bhadra Plaza

6 Bhadra Fort

7 Himabhai Institute

8 Electricity House

9 Mangaldas House

10 Sidi Saiyed Masjid

11 Central Bank of India

Walk 1

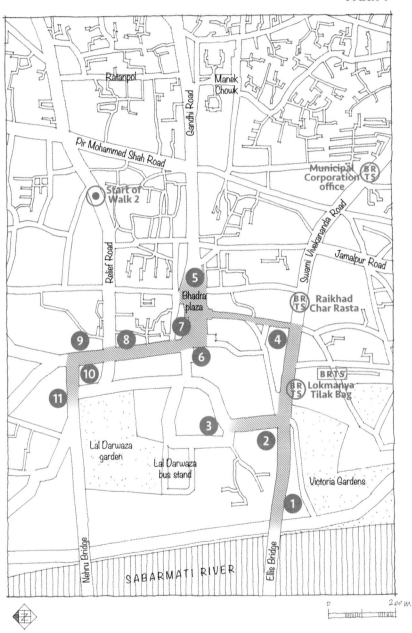

1 Manek Burj

Facing the river, Manek Burj was the foundation bastion of the city, laid down in 1411 by Ahmed Shah I. The tower was part of fortifications that enclosed the entire Bhadra fort. Originally, there was a stepwell located within the tower, but it dried up sometime in the nineteenth century and it was eventually refilled in 1866. The stepwell was part of a system that provided water to the city. A Persian wheel was stationed here to channel water from the river to the Bhadra Palace and other royal institutions. In 1869, the Ellis Bridge, the first bridge across the river was constructed near the bastion. This wooden bridge was replaced with an arched truss bridge with steel imported from Birmingham, England, in 1892 by architect Rao Himmatlal and the bastion was used as the foundation for the improvised structure. The tower can be entered on the same level as the bridge if the gate is open. The bridge was declared a heritage monument in 1989. In 1997, a newer concrete bridge was added after which the original bridge was closed to traffic.

2 Ahmed Shah Masjid

Opening times: daily, dawn to dusk (closed during prayers)
Admission: free

Leaving Manek Burj, follow the main road for about 250 metres and take a left. After about 50 metres you will come to the Ahmed Shah Masijd on your left. Built in 1414, a mere three years after the founding of the city, this impressive mosque is the oldest in Ahmedabad. As such, it reflects an early phase of the Indo-Saracenic building tradition in India. Because Islamic rule had only been recently established in India, the Muslim supervisors had to employ Hindu craftsmen. The general plan and orientation of the mosque, and specific elements like the minarets, are typically Muslim, but the carvings and structural elements contain a strong Hindu influence. The mosque's 152 pillars were recycled from a Hindu temple that used to stand on the site. The mosque is situated close to the Bhadra fort because it was used by the royal family for private worship. The mosque originally contained two minarets, one on either side of its entrance, but these collapsed in the earthquake of 1819; only their buttresses remain. Light enters the mosque via a series of stone screens located at the higher levels of the central bay as well as the lower levels of the side roofs. (Do remember to remove your shoes before entering the mosque and also to cover your head and knees.)

3 Congress Bhavan

Just north of the mosque, towards a rather chaotic T-junction, stands the **Martyrs of the Mahagujarat Movement statue**. After Independence, large parts of Gujarat became part of the bilingual state of Bombay (now Mumbai), while Saurashtra and Kutch became independent

states. This remnant from colonial times created great frustration among the Gujarati-speaking people and they demanded one state for all Gujaratis. In 1960 their call was acknowledged by the Central government and the separate states of Gujarat and Maharashtra were created. Directly behind the statue stands the **house of Sardar Patel**, one the leaders of the Independence movement and an early member of the Indian National Congress. Born in 1875 in the countryside of Gujarat, he moved to Ahmedabad to actively participate in politics and won in a municipal election to serve the municipality from 1922 to 1928. The house is a simple pitched-roof two-storey wooden form. It has a shaded walkway on its second floor, supported by simple wooden brackets. Sardar Patel actually never owned the house but rented it because he did not believe that owning property would help him achieve the goals he had set himself. Diagonally opposite the house of Sardar Patel stands the **Congress Bhavan**. The Gujarat unit of the Congress Committee was established here in 1920, with Sardar Patel as its first president. This office was the headquarters of the Indian National Congress party from 1930 onwards and played an important role in India's independence movement. The three-storey brick building has large protruding eaves to protect it against the sun, and added balustrades on the top floor, which give the building a somewhat art deco look. The central portion is open and the columns were made to resemble the Sultanate architectural style. Directly behind the Congress Bhavan stands the modern **State Bank of India**, designed in 1964 by Ahmedabad-based architect Hasmukh Patel. This head office was one of the first high-rise buildings in the city. It was also one of the first in Ahmedabad to be constructed using a reinforced-concrete framework and to have air-conditioning. The bank lobby features an interesting collection of artefacts relating to business and finance from the earliest days of the bank's existence.

4 Irish Presbyterian Mission High School

Head back to the main road and turn left and you will see the **Church of North India**. The simple cross-shaped church is the oldest surviving in Ahmedabad. Notable features are the large gothic windows, especially on the front facade, which is completely circular. Directly behind the church stands the Irish Presbyterian Mission High School. This long, low red-brick structure was one of the first colonial buildings to be constructed in Ahmedabad. The gothic windows hint at the religious background of the building while the beautifully carved wooden details are clearly a more local influence. The Presbyterian Church had started its missionary work in India from the 1840s, founding schools in villages throughout Gujarat. By 1863 the mission had come to Ahmedabad under the leadership of Dr James Glasgow, who had been in India since 1840. Under him they commissioned architect Rao Himmatlal, who worked for the British Public Works Department and is also credited with designing the steel replacement Ellis Bridge, to design this building complex. The Presbyterian mission was one of the many Christian missions in India. In fact, so many different Christian institutions were founded in the first half of the twentieth century that the wish arose to unify all Indian Christian missions into one Church Union. Finally, in 1970, all churches decided to continue as the Church of North India or C.N.I. for short. The school here in Ahmedabad is currently managed by the Gujarat Christian society, which also takes care of another 62 institutions throughout the state.

5 Bhadra Plaza

Turn left at the intersection just before the BRTS station and head north towards the recently redeveloped Bhadra plaza. This space is the proverbial heart of the city. When Ahmed Shah founded Ahmedabad in 1411 he conceived a central space, or *maidan*, to serve as a market place for the city. The Maidan-e Shah originally extended from the Bhadra fort to Teen Darwaza and was much wider than it is now. After hundreds of years the space of the *maidan* had slowly become encroached upon by surrounding buildings but also by hawkers and, more recently, cars. In recent decades, attention has begun to be paid to the condition of the plaza and has even led to the eventual redevelopment of the plaza. Executed under the supervision of B.V. Doshi, an important Indian architect well-known for his contributions to South-Asian architecture, Bhadra plaza is now once again a pedestrian zone, retaining space for hawkers and other commercial activities. Some buildings were demolished to open up the vista towards Teen Darwaza and a fountain was added. In the centre of the plaza **a statue of Chinubhai Ranchhodlal**, the first Hindu ever to receive a baronetcy from the British crown, stands proud. Chinubhai was the adopted grandson of the first mill owner in Ahmedabad and after he inherited the family's possessions in 1901 he continued to manage the company while also donating money to various institutions, most notably Gujarat University. This statue, located at the heart of the city, is a tribute to his efforts and was unveiled by Mahatma Gandhi in 1933. (Chinubhai also built an enormous mansion alongside the Sabarmati, which can be visited in the Shahibaug Walk.) Facing Bhadra plaza from the southern side is **Premabhai Hall**, which was designed as a theatre in 1975 by B.V. Doshi. The ground floor was intended to house an information centre with the main auditorium above. The building is of exposed concrete, following the construction methods Doshi learned while working for Le Corbusier. The hall is home to the Gujarat Vidyasabha, a performing arts institution of national repute. Currently closed, there are efforts to reopen the building in the near future.

6 Bhadra Fort

Opening times: daily, dawn to dusk
Admission: free

The western edge of Bhadra plaza is dominated by the Bhadra fort, which takes its name from Bhadra Kali, the clan goddess of the Solankis who first established this city as their capital. There is a shrine dedicated to the goddess in front of the fort, but this was built later, during the Maratha rule. This entire royal complex was originally much larger, and the brick structure that survives is merely a remnant, much reduced in size. The original building had a number of structures added to it over the years. To the left of the main entrance is the **Azam Khan Sarai**, built by the Mughal governor of Ahmedabad in 1637. Azam Khan ruled the city from this palace till his death in 1644. The fort itself was

also an addition to the original building; the clock over the main gate was added by the British and gives the tower an incongruous look, almost as if an English country church tower has been grafted onto an ancient Oriental structure. Currently the fort is undergoing renovation but it is still possible to enter. Do so via the main gate and turn left and you will find a staircase (workers on the site will be happy to guide you towards it if you cannot find it—in return for a small fee). From the roof of the fort you will be able to enjoy lovely views of the plaza and of this part of the city. The rear of the fort faces some other British colonial-era structures.

7 Himabhai Institute

Opening times: daily, 10am to 5pm
Admission: free

Slightly hidden behind trees and a cluster of hawkers directly across the plaza from Premabhai Hall stands Ahmedabad's first library, the Himabhai Institute, dating from 1851. One of the people involved in the establishment of the library was the Gujarati poet Kavi Dalpatram, whose statue stands in the nearby Kalupur area. He also helped form the Gujarat Vernacular Society, of which the library became a natural extension. The library is, however, named after Nagarsheth Himabhai Vakhatchand who donated a considerable amount towards its construction. The building itself is a simple two-storey structure with a series of arched windows. There is a reading room on the ground floor, which gives access to a courtyard behind. Judging by its current stock of books, the library has lost some of its former glory.

8 Electricity House

Leave Bhadra plaza by following the lane next to the library in a northerly direction and you will pass under a ceremonial metal gate. After this you will need to walk about 200 metres until you come to a large intersection. Although swarming with roaring buses and rickshaws, this plaza is home to no less than four marvellous buildings. The first is Electricity House, on the right-hand corner of Relief Road. This building was home to the Ahmedabad Electrical Company, which was in charge of providing electricity to the whole city. Claude Bartley, an English-born Mumbai-based architect, designed the building in a distinctive art deco style. Characteristic elements such as the lettering on the facade have survived to this day.

9 Mangaldas House

Opening times: daily, 7am to 11pm (for dining at Agashiye rooftop restaurant pre-booking is recommended)
Admission: free
www.houseofmg.com
+91-79-25506946

Another of the important buildings overlooking this busy intersection is Mangaldas House (also known as the House of M.G.) which sits opposite the Sidi Saiyed Masjid and is as much an architectural exhibit as a showcase for Ahmedabadi family history. The building's story starts at the end of the nineteenth century, when Mr Mangaldas and his brother were working their way up the ranks in one of Ahmedabad's many textile mills. Starting as a store-keeper, Mangaldas later acquired the mill and started building a textile empire. With their newly gained money and influence they decided to build a new house for their family in 1904. As the family expanded, another wing was added in 1924, giving the house its current form. By 1950 most members of the family had acquired their own bungalows in other parts of the city and it was decided to sub-let the mansion and use it for office purposes. This situation lasted till 1994, at which point the building had severely deteriorated. It was then decided to renovate the building and transform it into a heritage hotel, which opened in 2007. (The Mangaldas family has also been involved in the renovation of the Mangaldas Haveli which is featured in the Raipur Walk.) The Mangaldas

House is constructed in a neoclassical style using alternating white and red stone. The building is covered in elaborate pilasters and plaster medallions. Probably because it was constructed in two different phases, the building is quite asymmetrical. It is possible to wander around the ground-floor level of the hotel. The building is not only worthwhile for its architecture, but also for the food served here. There are two excellent restaurants—one downstairs and one on the rooftop—that serve traditional Gujarati *thali*s and other Indian dishes.

⑩ Sidi Saiyed Masjid

Opening times: daily, dawn to dusk (closed during prayers)
Admission: free

The third important building overlooking this junction is a small mosque constructed at the end of the Gujarat Sultanate in 1575 and originally part of the Bhadra fortifications. The main feature of the mosque—and an absolute must-see—is the stunning *jaali*s that make up the eastern facade containing the *mihrab*, especially the one containing a finely carved vine-and-palm motif that has gained nationwide fame. The motif has become the unofficial logo of Ahmedabad and has also served as the inspiration for the logo of Indian Institute of Management, Ahmedabad. Being one of the last mosques constructed in Ahmedabad it represents the final evolution of Sultanate architecture in the city.

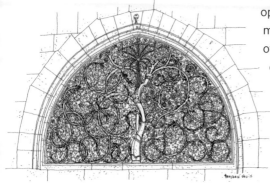

The front facade is completely opened up by moving the minarets to the corners of the building and using only arches to hold up the domed roof. Before the A.S.I. (Archaeological Survey of India) restored the building, it was in pretty bad shape, perhaps partly because the British had used it as administrative offices during their long occupation. Sidi Saiyed was a slave of Ahmed Shah. Although there were many slaves in the service of Shah, it is a little-known fact that Sidi Saiyed was of African descent. The Siddi community came to India in the sixteenth century from the East Africa coast. At this time, coastal Africa had large Muslim communities and trade between the various Muslim sultanates in Africa, Arabia and India was intensifying. Several Siddis rose to powerful positions within the Gujarati court. Nowadays, there is only a small group of around a 100 Siddis left in Ahmedabad. They still, however, continue some of their native cultural traditions, like the Dharmaal dance.

⑪ Central Bank of India

Finally, on the north side of the busy junction is the imposing multi-storey mass that houses the head office of the Central Bank of India, which was constructed in 1966. This reinforced-concrete building is divided into a broad podium containing banking facilities, and a six-level tower with offices. The external facade continues for another two floors on top of the offices, creating a roof garden. The building was designed by architect B.V. Doshi, who also designed the nearby Premabhai Hall at Bhadra plaza, and the massive brises-soleils on the office floors are very like the ones he has used for the CEPT building (which can be seen in the University Walk). These were of course also used by Doshi's famous teacher, Le Corbusier. The building originally had a finish of exposed concrete, but the facade has been whitewashed in later years. Doshi had a much grander vision for the building, and the public plaza above the first two banking floors—these were supposed to be part of a wider network of elevated public spaces and pedestrian bridges which was never completed.

Link to the Around Jama Masjid Walk:
Continue walking along Relief Road towards the intersection with Pir Mohammed Shah Road.

Around Jama Masjid

The Jama Masjid is located at the very heart of the old walled city of Ahmedabad. When it was built it was the biggest mosque in India. The Jama Masjid and adjacent tombs represent some of the earliest examples of Indo-Islamic architecture on the entire Indian subcontinent. The mosque was not only the religious centre of the Gujarat Sultanate, but the surrounding areas also served as the commercial hub of the city. The north-south trading routes from Delhi to the coast cross the imperial axis between Bhadra fort and the Jama Masjid. Thus, the alleys around the mosque are home to some of the most thriving markets and every lane specializes in a different commodity. All these attractions, combined with the winding narrow streets and laneways, with their constant hustle and bustle, makes it by far the liveliest and busiest part of the city.

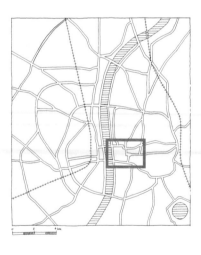

Key

1. Old Civil Hospital
2. New Education School
3. Hazrat Mohammad Shah Library
4. Jama Masjid
5. Teen Darwaza
6. Magen Abraham Synagogue
7. Parsi Fire Temple
8. Cloth and Food Markets
9. Manek Chowk
10. Badshah no Hajiro and Rani no Hajiro

Walk 2

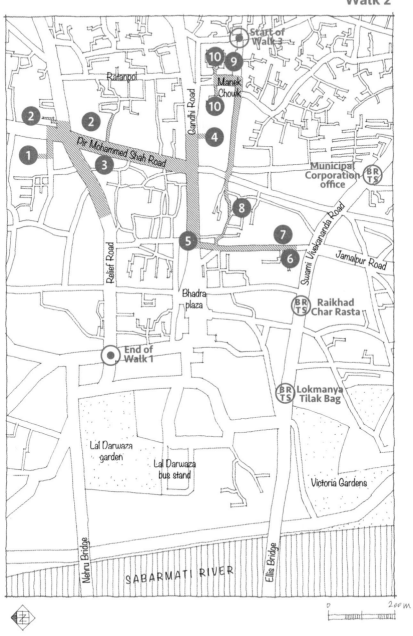

1 Old Civil Hospital

To find the Old Civil Hospital follow Relief Road to the intersection with Pir Mohammed Shah Road. Turn onto Gheekanta Road and turn left immediately and you will arrive at this former hospital. Although some earlier buildings might have existed from 1841 onwards, the hospital officially opened in 1858. It was largely funded by private donations from people such as Hutheesing, a wealthy Jain merchant, and Premabhai, a government official. Over the following decades several other wards and medical schools were added to the complex. With new public funds available from 1907 the current buildings were built, arranged around a large courtyard. It has a distinct red-and-white colour scheme, reminiscent of Mughal architecture. The ground floor has heavy-looking arches, while the first floor has a lighter wooden construction. After Independence, in 1949, the building was converted into a Collector's office. The New Civil Hospital opened its doors in 1953 in Shahibaug area, where ample land was available for a large campus. In 2000, the building here underwent another change as it was converted into a criminal court. If you visit during weekdays the hustle and bustle of advocates typing away on their typewriters will surely leave a lasting impression.

2 New Education School

Walk back to Relief Road. On your left you will notice some medieval-looking buttresses. Turn left twice to find the entry to **Hazrat Chhota Masjid**. Tucked away behind all the commercial development stands a tranquil tomb in the midst of trees. The open pillared tomb has an elegant dome. Opposite the mosque, facing Relief Road, stands the **New Education School**. This building dates from 1937 and was founded by Vasudevbhai Trivedi who trained as an educator and was a private tutor to the children of the Sarabhai family. The school is still run by his children and grandchildren. The windows on the facade sport a number of iron swans. The swan is the vehicle of Saraswati, the goddess of knowledge and the arts and a companion of Lord Brahma.

AROUND
JAMA MASJID

Due to safety precautions, admission is restricted for the general public/visitors. Another school, the **New High School**, stands to the rear of the New Education School. To reach it, follow Pir Mohammed Shah Road southwards and take a left turn after about 100 metres. Unlike the New Education School, the classrooms here are not arranged inside a single building, but are organized, rather, in three low-rise buildings, with open hallways facing other classrooms. The halls have iron balustrades running along their entire length. The school was built in 1926 by Harilal Bapulal Kapadia (who lived from 1893 to 1967) but had to be closed in 2012 because of lack of students. Part of the building now functions as a section of a private college.

Hazrat Chhota Masjid
Opening times: daily, dawn to dusk
Admission: free

3 Hazrat Mohammad Shah Library

Opening times: daily, 11am to 5pm (except Sundays)
Admission: free

Head back to Pir Mohammed Shah Road and you will see the lofty entrance to the Hazrat Mohammad Shah Library straight in front of you. This busy shopping street seems an odd place to find this charming stone building with its two small minarets on top. The entrance gate offers a clue to the age of the building as it is placed within a recessed space called a *diwan*. This architectural concept is native to Iran and is part of the architectural language the Mughals introduced to India. As you pass through the gate—after removing your shoes—you will find yourself in a wide courtyard. The building to the left is the tomb of Pir Mohammed Shah, who died here in 1749. This heavy-looking building is constructed in a classical Mughal style, recognizable by its distinctive use of colour, simple geometric ornamentation and ornamental arches. The tomb was erected during the reign of Aurangzeb, while the city was under Mughal rule, and this was only a few years before Ahmedabad finally fell into the hands of the Maratha Empire in 1757. The building to the right is the mosque, which, like the tomb, is mostly constructed in red sandstone. The inner facade resembles an older architectural style and it is possible that older elements have been re-used or re-assembled to construct the existing building. The ablution pond features a rectangular platform for people to sit and enjoy the cooling effect of the water. The complex extends to the rear where there are some hostels arranged around a number of courtyards. The construction of the complex began in the second half of the eighteenth century, after Pir Muhammad Shah had passed away. During his lifetime, Mohammad had gained influence as a religious scholar, poet and Sufi preacher. Originally from Bijapur in South India he moved to Ahmedabad in 1711 and started collecting books and manuscript in Arabic, Persian, Urdu and other languages. After his death the books were kept safe and eventually a library (or *kutubkhana*) was founded. The library can be accessed via a flight of stairs next to the main entrance. It now has over 20,000 books, including some rare manuscripts which are several hundred years old. The glass cases at the back of the library show Pir Mohammed Shah's original robes. Another case shows a selection of valuable manuscripts. Note that one manuscript can be read horizontally as well as vertically because the central banner contains the entire Koran fitted into the larger letters of the first lines of the Koran. They are written by the famous Iranian mathematician and astrologer

Al-Beruni who lived from 973 to 1048 AD. He was part of the great translation movement in the golden age of Islam that aimed to translate important books from Greek, Latin, Chinese and Indian languages into Arabic. The documents on display here were all translated from Sanskrit into Arabic and deal mainly with astronomy and consist of some of the most exceptional documents in the collection.

Hazrat Mohammad Shah Mosque
Opening times: daily, dawn to dusk
Admission: free

4 Jama Masjid

Opening times: daily, dawn to dusk (closed during prayers)
Admission: free

Continue along Pir Mohammed Shah Road for about 300 metres to the south and you will reach the busy intersection with Gandhi Road. Turn left and after about 100 metres you will be at the Jama Masjid. This entire mosque is surrounded by shops so its entrance, which is on the right-hand side, can be easy to miss. Once you enter the mosque it shuts off much of the street noise, adding to the

atmosphere of serenity to be found here. The entire complex is built of sandstone and when it was completed in 1424, after a decade of construction, it was the largest mosque on the Indian subcontinent (currently the Jama Masjid in New Delhi holds that title). As the Friday Mosque it is also the most important mosque in the city and was used by the kings for their Friday prayers. The mosque is planned around a large courtyard, featuring an ablution tank in the centre and with the prayer hall facing west towards Mecca. There are entrances at all cardinal directions, but the southern one is most important. The facade of the prayer hall contains three main arches, elevated above the other parts of the mosque. The central one was originally flanked by minarets but these collapsed in the earthquake of 1819 and were never rebuilt. The interior has an impressive number of pillars, 260 to be precise, set in a tight grid. The *qibla* wall features five marble *mihrab*s, one for each dome. The space to the right-hand side is reserved for women, while the stone screens enable them to hear the sermon while maintaining their separation from the men as they pray. Upon exiting the mosque, walk back towards the intersection with Pir Mohammed Shah Road. The second building from the corner, on the left-hand side, is one of the several old libraries located in this part of the city. Called **Dadabhai Naoroji Library**, it dates from 1930 and is constructed in a plain colonial style, with tall pilasters reaching the entire height of the building.

5 Teen Darwaza

Head back to the junction with Pir Mohammed Shah Road and continue to walk along Gandhi Road in the direction of the Teen Darwaza gates that will rise up in front of you above the crowd. Teen Darwaza literally means 'three gates' and it was originally the entrance to the Bhadra complex. Constructed during the reign of Ahmed Shah, this gate is one of the oldest buildings still standing in Ahmedabad. The central arch is slightly wider than the two adjoining ones and is decorated with carved buttresses. The gate is topped by a three-metre-high parapet, with three protruding *jharoka*s (overhanging balcony) enclosing a terrace.

This terrace originally had a wooden roof but this was removed in 1877. The space around the gate is occupied by hawkers.

6 Magen Abraham Synagogue

Opening times: closed, but can be opened by the caretaker
Admission: free

Continue along the alley that heads south just behind the gate and, with some agility required, you will reach a slightly wider lane where you will need to turn right for a few metres. A main road will open out in front of you; this is where you will have to turn left and head south for about 200 metres where you will come to the Magen Abraham Synagogue. This is the only synagogue in the state of Gujarat. It was established in 1934, before which the Jewish community used a small prayer hall nearby. The synagogue was funded by donations from within the Indian Jewish community and built by a French architect.

The three-bay building is constructed in a simple art deco style. The front of the building houses an office and stairs lead to the second floor. Behind this lies the main prayer hall. Women occupy the balconies on the second floor. The rear of the building contains the holy scripture of the Jews, the Thora, written in Hebrew. The paper of the Thora is sacred and not to be touched by anyone (hence the use of wooden rollers) and this particular one is around 250-years old. India has had Jews living here since ancient times, but the Ahmedabadi Jewish community is most likely to have descended from immigrants from the Middle East. During the sixteenth century, large parts of the Middle East came under Ottoman control. Jews fled religious persecution to trading ports like Bangkok and Shanghai in China, as well as Bombay and Surat in India. The Jewish community were mainly traders and followed this activity along the networks of the European trading companies. In recent years many Indian Jews have migrated to America or Israel and at present only around 140 Jews remain in Ahmedabad. As the synagogue is scarcely used anymore, issues of religious insecurity have come to the fore, with the result that it is only possible to enter the building by contacting the caretaker who lives to the rear. If he is in, he will gladly take you around the building.

7 Parsi Fire temple

Just opposite the Magen Abraham Synagogue is the Vakil Anjuman Adran, an *agiyari* or Parsi Fire Temple. This is one of the two fire temples in Ahmedabad. Parsi literally means Persian, but is used to denote the Zoroastrian refugees of religious persecution who fled from modern-day Iran to India during the eighth to tenth centuries. Until the beginning of the nineteenth century not that many Parsis actually lived in Ahmedabad, but with the booming of the textile industry many were attracted from cities like Bombay. In 1896 one Parsi, Dhanjibhai Midara, even managed to establish his own mill and two years later another Parsi-owned textile business opened. The community prospered, but even before that the first fire temple was opened in 1846. Disaster hit in 1975 when it flooded, so a new one was built in 1977 and subsequent buildings have been added to the complex. Standing in the small forecourt are two buildings: the one to the left is the Parsi Panchayat, which contains administration and management; the one to the front is the fire temple. Prayers take place here on auspicious days based on the 360-day Parsi calendar. Entrance to non-Parsis is restricted. Both buildings are built from brick and have a pitched roof. Despite the lack of any obvious decoration, the buildings look altogether quite pleasant. India has around 60,000 Parsis, and the Parsi community in Ahmedabad numbers around 1,750.

8 Cloth and Food Markets

Head back over the road and retrace your steps back up the alley you came down earlier but now follow it all the way to where it opens up to the main road. The whole area around Bhadra plaza buzzes with people and has been a market ever since the foundation of the city. Certain specific types of goods are usually organized around a single street or alley and the sheer variety and amount of things on offer attracts people from all over the city. There are separate markets for cloth, saris, jewellery, utensils, shoes, food and more. This particular area is known as the **cloth market** and it is one of the best places in the city to buy garments. After about 50 metres you will come to the entrance of the historical **fruit market**. This is where most of the city's fruit sellers are located; it can be difficult to make out the architecture behind the vibrant bustle but it is worth the effort to stop and try and take a look. Spices are sold in the shops on the left while hawkers sell seasonal fruit on the street.

9 Manek Chowk

Follow the market roadway until you reach a busy T-junction and enter Manek Chowk. This is another busy market square (or *chowk*), specializing in gold and silver. At night, the square transforms into a wonderful place to have snacks with a series of eateries springing

up as the evening cools down. This square is named after local saint Baba Maneknath, who, according to legend, lived here before the city was founded. When Ahmed Shah decided to settle here, his efforts of building the city during the day would be mysteriously demolished at night. The story goes that while the walls were being constructed Baba would weave a blanket and as he unravelled it every night the city walls would fall apart. Ahmed Shah discovered this and agreed to name this place in his memory on the condition that Baba would stop his unravelling of the city walls. Just around the corner from Manek Chowk is the former building of the **Ahmedabad Stockbrokers' Association**. Following the industrial boom of the textile mills in the second half of the nineteenth century, a stock exchange was founded in 1894. The present three-storey building dates from 1919 and is constructed in an enthusiastically florid neoclassical style. There are some recognizably Indian elements contained in the facade, such as the five *jharoka*s on the upper two floors, although these are also executed in a neoclassical style. The building no longer houses the stock exchange, which is now housed in a new building close to the university. Opposite it is one of Ahmedabad's first housing clusters, **Muhurat Pol**. Now largely occupied by silversmiths, it is well worth a visit.

⑩ Badshah no Hajiro and Rani no Hajiro

Opening times: daily, dawn to dusk
Admission: free

Manek Chowk provides access to the royal tombs. Follow the alley on the western side of the square and you will find the tomb of city-founder Ahmed Shah, which is known as **Badshah no Hajiro**. The tomb was constructed in 1446 in the same architectural style as the Jama Masjid. The two monuments are actually right next to each other, although the entrance is barred. The plan of the tomb is symmetrical, with a passage running around the central area which houses the marble tomb of Ahmed Shah. Each side of it has a protruding portico, although only the southern one provides an entrance. Ahmed Shah's son, Muhammed Shah, and grandson, Qutbuddin Ahmed Shah, are buried alongside him. On the other side of Manek Chowk is the tomb of Ahmed Shah's three wives. Known as **Rani no Hajiro**, it is similar in size and style to the king's tomb and also has the structure of a courtyard. The queens' tomb, however, has been heavily encroached upon, with some of its steps having been used as useful home extensions.

Link to Raipur Walk:
Follow Madan Gopal ni Haveli Marg until you come to the Dastoor Khan Masjid.

Raipur

The Raipur neighbourhood lies directly south-east of the central market area of the city. This is an excellent place to explore the traditional lanes and townhouses of Ahmedabad. The townhouses—or *havelis*—are courtyard houses that are perfectly adapted to the local climate and cultural traditions. The houses are organized in long winding lanes that can be locked with a fortified gate, or *pol*. These communities came about mostly during the turbulent eighteenth century, when the Muslim Mughals were challenged by the Maratha power. Distinct communities, sharing caste, religion and occupation, felt the need to protect themselves during the periods of war, raids and communal violence. In all, the old city of Ahmedabad has around 60,000 houses organized in more than 600 *pol*s. Raipur is also home to many Hindu temples, including some that were built here by the Maratha Empire, during their occupation of the city.

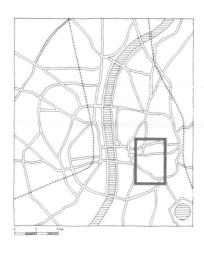

Key

1. City Heritage Centre
2. Mangaldas Haveli
3. Rameshwar Mandir
4. Madan Gopal ni Haveli
5. Dastoor Khan Masjid
6. Tomb of Rani Sipri
7. Dwarkadhish Mandir
8. Desai ni Pol
9. Hatkeshwar Mandir
10. Moto Suthar no Vado
11. Shankar Vyas Haveli

Walk 3

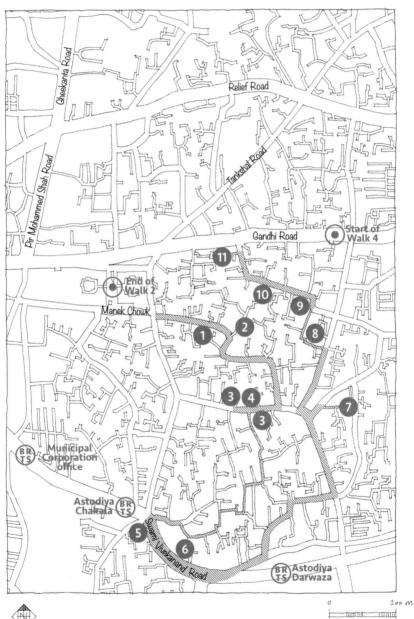

① City Heritage Centre

Opening times: daily, 9am to 2pm and 6 to 11pm
Admission: free (knock on the front door and report to reception)
www.cityhc.org
+91 79 2214 0830

From Manek Chowk, walk east towards Lakha Patel ni Pol. Along the main road of this *pol*, on the right-hand side, stands the Diwanji ni Haveli that houses the City Heritage Centre. This NGO was established in 2006 by a number of enthusiastic engineers with the purpose of putting a halt to the dramatic decay of heritage structures in the old city of Ahmedabad. The centre has been involved in various projects across the old city, for example Mehta House and the Kala Ramji Mandir (both of which are included in this walk). The NGO provides know-how on how to successfully preserve the *haveli*s, as exemplified in their own office at Diwanji ni Haveli. One of the key issues in the restoration of the *haveli*s is their sagging wooden structures. In this one, all the wooden joints have been replaced and the original, heavier, floor of fuska wood replaced by a lighter variant. This enormous four-storey *haveli* was the home of the *diwan* (or minister) of the Mughal governor of Ahmedabad. The building is thought to date from the middle of the eighteenth century. Its main entrance is on a high plinth, on which a series of stately wooden columns support a large balcony on the first floor. The columns are supported by stone bases, with the outer ones showing wrestling figures. The various rooms, halls and wings of the building are essentially interlocked around the central courtyard. The courtyard is finished in similar fashion to the front facade, with a simple carved wooden structure and plaster decorations. From the courtyard it is possible to enter the water tank below the house. Although no longer in use, it is one of the few places in the old city where the tank of the traditional water-harvesting system can be accessed. Upstairs you will find a series of rooms which still contain many of their original features, such as the stained glass and plasterwork. From the roof you will have a nice view of this part of the old city.

2 Mangaldas Haveli

Opening times: daily, 9am to 2pm and 6 to 11pm
Admission: free

Continue walking for another 50 metres or so until you come at a T-junction where you should take a left onto Lakha Patel ni Pol. The fourth building on the right is the Mangaldas Haveli, a three-storey house renovated by the Mangaldas family in 2006. This 200-year-old house was originally inhabited by an influential Brahmin family, who have long since moved out. The *haveli* is beautifully restored and allows you to see the way a Gujarati house was traditionally organized. The ground floor is divided into three segments by a central courtyard open to the sky. The inside of the courtyard has intricate wooden carving of a green-and-white floral pattern. The teak for this house was imported from Myanmar, which was part of the British Empire from 1824 onwards. During the monsoon, the rain simply falls right into the courtyard and the water is collected. All *haveli*s in Ahmedabad originally had rainwater harvesting systems that allowed each family to collect water

during the monsoon. In the corner, near the stairs, it is possible to look into the 15-metre-deep well, from which water could be collected. The stairs take you to the first floor which functioned as the main living room. The mosaics on the floor are imported from Italy and there is stained glass all along the top of the windows of the front facade. If you peek out of the window you can see the **Divitia Haveli**, which stands directly opposite. It is possible to imagine how people use to talk from building to building across the narrow alley. The house was intended to function as a restaurant but due to local municipal parking restrictions the restaurant was not allowed to open. A heritage walk is organized daily at 10 pm and lasts an hour in which you are shown around the local area by a local guide who explains some of the fascinating aspects of traditional *pol* life in Ahmedabad.

3 Rameshwar Mandir

Head back to the main lane and follow its winding course for around 400 metres until you come to a T-junction and turn right. This road has two temples close to one another; they are called Rameshwar Mandir and Kameshwar Mandir respectively. The Marathas ruled Ahmedabad from 1758 to 1817 and during their rule they built various temples in the city. The maximum extent of the Maratha Empire encompassed the entire region of central India, from the Arabian Sea to the Bay of Bengal. Their rule was marked by constant warfare, first with various sultanates and the Mughal Empire, and later with the British. All temples built in Ahmedabad by the Marathas are dedicated to the god Shiva, including the two here. Shiva is one of the three main deities in the Hindu pantheon and became particularly popular during Maratha rule because of the dynasty's founder Shivaji. Shivaji was born in Pune district, of Maharashtra state, and was named after Shiva. During the seventeenth century he successfully rebelled against the Muslim sultanate of Bijapur and established a Hindu state. The temples are as a result both a tribute to Lord Shiva and to Shivaji, as well as a projection of Maratha power. Rameshwar and Kameshwar are names for different forms of Shiva. An easy way to identify any Shiva temple is by the presence of Nandi, the bull that serves as Shiva's mount. The larger Rameshwar Mandir (on the right-hand side) has a classic two-tiered system of pavilion or vestibule in front and a towering *shikhara* behind. The *shikhara* contains the *garbha griha*, the room that holds the deity. The Kameshwar Mandir (on the left-hand side of the road) is smaller. Unfortunately, both temples are in a bad state of disrepair.

4 Madan Gopal ni Haveli

In between the two temples stands the beautiful Madan Gopal ni Haveli, which is difficult to miss with its enormous 50-metre-long wooden facade. The house is divided into four units, each one slightly protruding further

out than its neighbour. The left-most unit is the only three-storey part of the house and is extremely intricately carved. The bottom beam features miniature elephant heads, while the other woodwork has floral motifs. This part of the house acted as the main entrance, impressing visitors as they moved inside; the other part of the building is finished relatively simply, with brownish plaster in-between the wooden structure. The house belongs to the Sarabhai family, who have played an important role in establishing prosperous industries and institutions in Ahmedabad. One of the people who grew up here was Mridula Sarabhai, sister of Vikram Sarabhai. She was born in 1911 and already at the age of 19 became involved in India's freedom movement when she took part in the famous Salt March. The march was led by Mahatma Gandhi who intended to make salt at the coast in protest against the oppressive British salt tax laws. Mridula later became one of the general secretaries of the Indian National Congress party which ruled India for many years after Independence.

5 Dastoor Khan Masjid

Opening times: daily, dawn to dusk (closed during prayers)
Admission: free

Enter the *pol* directly opposite to the Madan Gopal ni Haveli. Follow it for 100 metres till you reach a flight of stairs. Continue for another 50 metres till you reach a traditional *chowk*, featuring a *chabutara* and a small temple. Take a right, follow the winding *pol* and take a left where the *pol* stops at a T-junction. Take a right and at the end of the *pol* another left. Follow the *pol* till it makes out all the way onto Swami Vivekananda Road. Overlooking the junction from a high plinth stands the

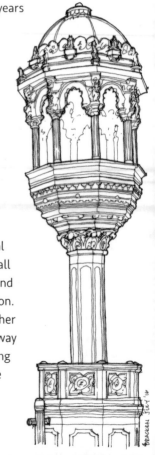

Dastoor Khan Masjid, named in honour of Dastoor Khan. It was constructed by Dastoor Khan sometime between 1463 and 1486. He was one the ministers during Mahmud Begada's long rule (1458–1511). You enter the mosque via a small protruding bay which brings you into a courtyard. All of the mosques built during Begada's reign show a degree of architectural experimentation and this mosque is in fact unique in a number of ways. Its plan is almost square, instead of rectangular; it has no minarets but has a vaulted corridor running along all sides of the courtyard instead. The facade of the mosque is entirely covered with stone screens or *jaali*s. Underneath the courtyard, and partly in the plinth, lies a large water tank that used to provide drinking water for the wider community. The water tank used to be open air and functioned as a small stepwell, but this has unfortunately been covered up by a new floor and a modern ablution tank. For whatever reason, this architectural experiment was not considered worthy as a template for the later city mosques, since no other mosque was built in the same manner.

6 Tomb of Rani Sipri

Opening times: daily, dawn to dusk
Admission: free

Opposite Dastoor Khan Masjid stands the elegant mosque and tomb of Rani Sipri which was built in 1514. Rani Sipri is thought to have been a wife of Mahmud Begada and the story goes that her young son, Abu Baqr, had committed some misdemeanour, after which Begada had him poisoned. Struck by grief, she commissioned the mosque. (Meanwhile, another son of Begada, Muzaffar II, succeeded Begada to the throne of Gujarat in 1511.) Although it was built only half a century later than Dastoor Khan Masjid, this mosque's style is quite unlike its older cousin. Their minarets are slender and placed at the far end of their front facades, while the side facades have beautifully carved *jharoka*s. The front facade is open but lacks the usual arches found in earlier mosques. The tomb itself contains the grave of Rani Sipri

and the columns in front of the tomb align with the mosque (quite an unusual feature, in fact). The central dome is raised above the rest of the structure. Carved stone *jaali*s, protruding eaves run along all four sides of the facade. The entrance steps are sculpted in the Hindu style, showing an abstraction of tiger and lotus motives that are also usually found in temples. These stylistic changes are all part of the architectural language that had matured during the reign of Mahmud Begada. The result is the classic Gujarati Indo-Saracenic architectural style; a perfect blend of both worlds.

7 Dwarkadhish Mandir

Opening times: daily, dawn to dusk
Admission: free

Just 50 metres beyond the Tomb of Rani Sipri stands the **Astodiya Darwaza**, which marks the extent of the old city. This gate is typical of those that used to surround the city. Continue walking along Swami Vivekananda Road for 150 metres and take a left. Follow the lane as it gently bends towards the right. Take a right till you come to a slightly wider main road. Take a left and after about 250 metres you will come on a busy junction. Take a right and immediately another right to enter the **Bauva ni Pol**. Head into this *pol* and you should see straight in front of you a beautiful three-storey heritage *haveli* decorated with neoclassical balustrades and iron brackets. Slightly further along is the entrance to the courtyard around which the **Dwarkadhish Mandir** is organized. Unlike previous temples, this one was commissioned by local people. It is dedicated to the god Krishna (Dwarkadhish being a name for Krishna, an incarnation of one of the main deities in Hinduism: Vishnu). The two main buildings in this temple complex are two *haveli*-like structures. On the left is a two-storey structure on a high plinth painted green. The ground floor has elaborately carved wooden brackets and the walls are decorated with wall paintings around the *otla*. The building on the right is three storeys high but sits on a much lower plinth and has dark brown brackets. The ceiling of the first-floor gallery is adorned with delicately carved floral motifs. The temple and school are managed by a community of Brahmins that still live within the complex. The temple is also home to several cows, which are of course sacred.

8 Desai ni Pol

Head back to the main road and take the lane that goes directly north just after the clock tower. Follow it for 150 metres and keep an eye out for the gate that leads to Desai ni Pol on the left-hand side of the road. Desai ni Pol is one of the best preserved clusters of *pol* houses in the city. Walk towards the centre of the *pol* at **Akha Bhagat Chowk** to get the best views of the buildings. The statue is of the Gujarati poet Akha Bhagat, who lived from 1591 to 1656. He lived in this *pol*, together with other members of the goldsmiths' community. His poetry was satirical in nature and was part of the Bhakti movement. This movement originated in Southern India and promoted a more individualistic approach to Hinduism. In the nineteenth century, the *pol* came to be known for the many residents who were involved in the Indian freedom movement. The *haveli* on the corner with green circle-shaped balustrades belonged to Chinubhai Baronet, the first Indian to receive a baronetcy from the British (his statue stands on Bhadra plaza). The *haveli* is interesting because of its use of iron. Opposite this house was the two-storey *haveli* with dark brown woodwork that belonged to his grandfather Ranchhodlal Chhotalal. Ranchhodlal was born in 1823 and in 1861 founded the first cotton mill in Ahmedabad (a second mill followed in 1872). These enterprises were successful and it allowed him to help fund the Gujarat College and the Victoria Jubilee Hospital. He was also the first Indian president of the municipality of Ahmedabad and it was he who started the underground drainage and water-supply network. The *haveli* currently houses **CHETNA** (Centre for Health, Education, Training and Nutrition Awareness) which helps to create awareness on health and nutrition issues. There are various other *haveli*s in this *pol* listed as heritage structures and worth a closer look.

9 Hatkeshwar Mandir

Opening times: daily, dawn to dusk
Admission: free

Exit Desai ni Pol at the other end and on your left-hand side, positioned on the corner stands the **Hatkeshwar Mandir**. This Maratha-era Shiva temple stands in the centre of the plot and is shielded from the road by two wooden *haveli*-like structures. The two-storey northern facade has three tiers of carved woodwork and has the appearance of a residence. The temple itself has the typical layout of most north-Indian temples and is representative of Solanki architecture. The cross-shaped *mandapa* houses the entrance and is decorated with *torana*s and dancing girls. The entrance pavilion provides access to the inner sanctum, or *garbha griha*, above which the carved *shikhara* is positioned. The building has recently been restored in collaboration between the local municipality and the Embassy of France.

10 Moto Suthar no Vado

Mehta Heritage Home
jagdipmehta@gmail.com
+91-98-25310315

Exit the Hatkeshwar Mandir via the northern entrance and take a left. Next door stands the heritage *haveli* belonging to Jivkar Somnathrupjidas, who lived here from 1927 to 1978. The three-storey house has a mix of colonial influences, including the European-inspired plinth with its oval windows and the gothic elements on the upper storeys. Continue to walk and after about 80 metres turn to second *pol* on the left. Facing the entrance of the *pol* stands the heritage home of Ashish Mehta. This three-storey house can be entered via the garden in front. The house was built in 1870 and has recently been completely restored with the financial assistance of the French government and the AMC Heritage Department. The Mehta family was able to connect two houses to form one single large one and refurbish all the elements within. The central *chowk* has Italian tiles and a *jhoola* (traditional hammock). Underneath the *chowk* is a large water tank which is still functional. The Mehta family runs a home-stay, which is located on the first floor. It has been adapted to fit a modern lifestyle, with toilets on each floor and a new light well. The lovely stained glass of the Mehta house has been preserved.

11 Shankar Vyas Haveli

Continue walking along the *pol*. Just before Gandhi Road, nestling on the left-hand side stands an exquisite three-storey *haveli*. The ground floor of the house is reached by ascending five steps, on either side of which are raised platforms, known as *otla*s, where people can sit. The first floor has five balconies surrounded by carvings of flowers and animals. Notably, elephants' trunks and several small birds are incorporated into the carvings. The *haveli* is around 200 years old and was originally owned by a cotton-mill owner. He started renting the house to a lawyer, Harish Shankar Reva Shankar Vyas, whose name is inscribed above the main door of the house. Incidentally, this man was also head of the Rashtriya Swayamsevak Sangh (RSS), Ahmedabad office, an organization started in 1925 in Nagpur with the aim of supporting Hindu nationalism. The organization was banned by the British but continued to remain active, even after Independence. The Indian government also, incidentally, banned them three times because their role in India remains controversial as they initially took inspiration from right-wing groups in Europe and have been accused of inciting violence against other religious groups (most notably the Babri Masjid demolition in 1992 and Mahatma Gandhi's assassination in 1948). The organization, however, is hugely popular, with over five million members and is a strong supporter of the Bharatiya Janata Party (BJP) who are often in government these days. Vyas used his house to organize RSS meetings and one of the people who came here was Narendra Modi, active with the RSS before he became the (BJP) chief minister of Gujarat and currently the prime minister of India;

little did Vyas know that some decades later a phone call to Modi would help to preserve this house. Maintenance of these old houses is expensive and until recently this one was in very bad condition. With a little help from Modi and a local NGO the house was stabilized and saved from demolition. If you ask nicely you might be able to enter and see some of the interior's features. Like all *havelis*, it is organized around a central courtyard. The floor of the courtyard is of Italian stone and there are Western-style frescoes adorning the sides and rear of the house.

Link to the Station Area Walk:
Head back to the main lane and turn left. Head to Gandhi Road and take a right and follow it for approximately 400 metres.

Station area

Nearest BRTS: Kalupur railway station
Walking time: 1 hours and 30 minutes

When the Ahmedabad railway station opened in 1863 a new era began for the city. The railway meant new and improved connections to the country's capital at Delhi, and also to the ports along the Indian Ocean. The station was built around 300 metres from the city gates, and the area in-between the city walls and the railway line was a logical place to settle for trading houses, hotels and postal services. A substantial number of buildings from this time have survived, although many have changed their function. Parts of this area had already been settled, and some of their landmarks, like the 'shaking minarets' still stand today. Unfortunately, not many people visit this part of the city, which is a pity because it has some wonderful architectural heritage.

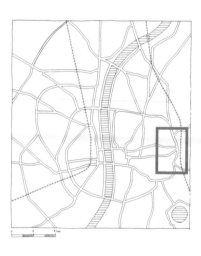

Key

1. Sambharnath Jain Temple
2. Amritvarshini Vav
3. Sidi Bashir Masjid
4. Victoria Jubilee Hospital
5. Shaking Minarets
6. Manilal Mansion
7. Maskati Market
8. Kalupur Darwaza
9. Manamiya Hava Tower

Walk 4

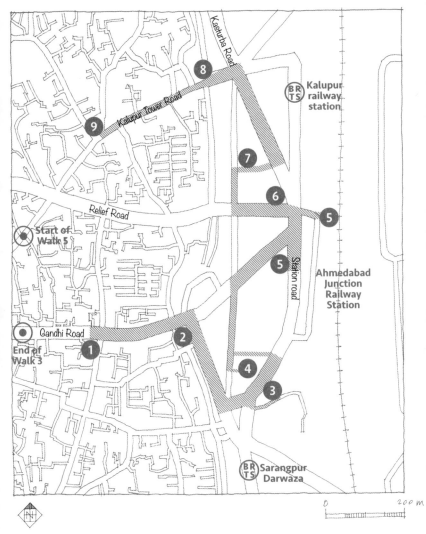

Kasturba Road

8

BR
TS Kalupur
railway
station

Kalupur Tower Road

9

7

6

Relief Road

5

Start of
Walk 5

5

Station road

Ahmedabad
Junction
Railway
Station

Gandhi Road

End of
Walk 3

1

2

4

3

BR
TS Sarangpur
Darwaza

N

0   200 m

① Sambharnath Jain Temple

Opening times: daily, dawn to dusk
Admission: free

Perched on the corner of Gandhi Road stands the Sambharnath Jain Temple. The ground floor of this two-storey place of worship contains shops, while the main idol is situated on the first floor. Because the building has been completely whitewashed it is difficult to differentiate between the wooden support structure and the slabs of marble in-between them. The facade is richly decorated with

various types of *torana*s, columns and capitals. If inspected closely, almost every element on the facade has figurines, both human and animal, incorporated within them. The temple is said to be around 400-years old.

2 Amritvarshini Vav

Opening times: daily, dawn to dusk
Admission: free

Follow Gandhi Road in an easterly direction for around 500 metres and you will reach the end of the walled city and notice the **Panchkuva Darwaza.** This city gate was not originally part of the city wall but was built in 1871 on the order of the British administration to provide better access to the train station. Unlike most Ahmedabad city gates, this one has three arches and its entire structure is elongated.

The gate takes its name from five nearby wells (or *vavs*). Just before the gate, on your right, is the entrance to **Amritvarshini Vav** (also known as Panchkuva Vav). Although not as old as, and indeed smaller in size than, Adalaj and Dada Hari *vavs*, this is significant because it is the only stepwell built within the walls of the old medieval city. It was built in 1723 during Mughal rule by the provincial governor of Gujarat, Raghunathdas. As the Mughal power was waning, the governor might have preferred the idea of having an extra source of water within the city walls. What also sets this stepwell apart from the others is its unusual L-shaped plan that leads down three flights of stairs to the circular well at the back. A characteristic of Mughal architecture is the use of arches (as opposed to the trabeated structure used in Adalaj) to deal with structural forces. Some conservation work has been carried out but you will probably still need to slip past the metal gate before entering.

3 Sidi Bashir Masjid

Opening times: daily, dawn to dusk
Admission: free

After passing under Panchkuva Darwaza, take a right and follow the edge of the walled city for 600 metres. On your right-hand side you will see another city gate, **Sarangpur Darwaza**. This is one of the original 12 gates built by Mahmud Begada in 1487 to defend the city. Sarangpur Darwaza's size and decorative elements are typical of these gates. The length of the walkway behind the battlements was over 10 kilometres, while the width of the wall was several metres thick and had 189 bastions and over 6,000 actual battlements. Despite these fortifications the city fell several times, first to the Mughals, then to the Maratha, and finally to the British. To continue, head towards the opposite side of the busy traffic junction in front of Sarangpur gate. Above a cluster of low-rise residential buildings, you will spot the towering minarets of **Sidi Bashir Masjid**. The original structure of the mosque was destroyed by the marauding Maratha army in 1753 but fortunately the minarets survive. The mosque and its minarets were originally constructed in 1452, most likely by the nobleman Malik Sarang, whose name is remembered in the Sarangpur neighbourhood and city gate. Yet the mosque is named after Sidi Bashir, a slave at Mahmud Begada's court who might have been involved in its construction. The minarets, with their carved balconies, are typical of the type known as 'shaking minarets' for their ability to survive earthquakes. Remarkably, they seem to be able to let the vibrations pass through them without actually collapsing. The technology for this seems to be traceable to Persia, where similar minarets were built. When the British took apart one of the minarets to try and find out its secrets they found they were unable to reconstruct it properly and so there is no guarantee that it still has its functioning shaking capabilities. (The clue to their remarkable ability to survive is probably due to the use of a particular type of sandstone used in the foundation and/or as layers in the towers but nobody seems to know for sure.)

4 Victoria Jubilee Hospital

Opening times: daily, dawn to dusk
Photography not allowed

Head back to the main road and take a right. After 100 metres, cross the road and enter the campus of the Victoria Jubilee Hospital. It was established in 1865 by mill owner Ranchhodlal as the first women's hospital in the city. The history of the building is tied up with its first director, and the first female doctor in the city, Motibai Kapadia. She obtained her degree in medicine in 1889 and headed the hospital for over 40 years. There are two historic buildings on the campus. Upon entering, on your right, the first building is the college of nursing for nurses and midwives. This two-storey brick building was built in 1905 and has a central porch with doric columns. The main building on the campus is the two-storey whitewashed hospital built in 1906 in a distinct neoclassical style. It contains space for 100 beds arranged along the arched verandas. It continues to operate as a public hospital and now treats both women and men. Leave the campus on the opposite side of the compound and on the adjacent plot of land, on your left-hand side, you will see a **community hall** built by

Doctor Kapadia in 1929. It is a small one-storey building in blue and yellow pastel colours and it also continues to function to this day.

5 Shaking Minarets

Head back to the main road and take a right. Follow the road for 200 metres and take another right. On the corner you will see the four-storey **Sri Dhanalakshmi Market** building, crowned with an ochre-coloured Indo-Saracenic dome. Looking down the road you can see that it is aligned with more **shaking minarets**; a subtle yet effective urban design element to integrate this part of the city with its surroundings. All remains of the mosque to which the minarets

belonged have vanished which means that nothing is known of its builder and it can only be dated based on the minarets' architectural style, which shows similarities to the nearby Sidi Bashir Masjid and Bibi ki Masjid, both of which were constructed in the early part of the sixteenth century. Both of these sandstone minarets have four balconies each and reach a height of more than 30 metres. They now find themselves within the confines of **Ahmedabad Station** (also known as Kalupur Railway Station), which was built in 1863 and first connected to the railway network the following year, when the line to Surat and Mumbai was opened. The connection greatly accelerated the development of the city. The booming textile business profited in particular, especially from the sharp reduction in cost and time of transportation. Of the original station building nothing is left; the present building is not really worth a visit. Directly opposite the railway station stands the old **Fanibunda** building. This three-storey, cream-coloured neoclassical building dates from 1926 and consists of three bays. The central one is accentuated by two double-storey pilasters, while inside, some of the original woodwork still remains. The ground floor is currently occupied by a post office.

6 Manilal Mansion

Head onto **Relief Road**, directly opposite to the shaking minarets. This road was carved out of the existing city in 1884 to provide, literally, relief to the traffic on Gandhi Road (which was only later renamed in honour of Mahatma Gandhi) and give direct access to the train station. Many buildings were destroyed during this process, so most of the buildings facing the road are indeed from after 1884. After about 50 metres, on your right-hand side, stands **Manilal Mansion**. Partly covered by ragtag advertisements, this building dates from 1913 and used to function as a *dharmashala* (or guest house) for Hindus visiting the city. It was built in the memory of Seth Manilal by three of his wives after he passed away. Seth Manilal was a prominent citizen who had donated land for the development of the first organized expansion of the city in Maninagar. The two-storey neoclassical building is made up of seven arched bays decorated with plaster motifs and some rather eccentric-looking capitals. Inside, there is a stately courtyard with a bust of Seth Manilal.

7 Maskati Market

Keep walking down Relief Road for another 100 metres and take a right. After 50 metres you will come to the Maskati market on your right. Built by Nemtullabai, one of the widows of Seth Maskati, the market consists of a series of internal lanes giving access to rows of two-storey shops. The Maskatis were a prominent family of Gujarati textile traders who traded their goods all over the world. Their export business was active in the Kingdom of Siam (now Thailand) where their textiles were known by the company name 'pha Maskati'. Cloth would come in from villages throughout Gujarat and, later, from the city's textile mills to be prepared here for export. Much of the trading empire collapsed in the twentieth century. The market here sells finished garments. Its buildings date from 1906 and have two ornate entrance gates which link the three bays of the market together. Many of the shops inside the market have been refurbished, but some do still have their original woodwork. You can walk through the Maskati market and exit via the gate on the other side. Head left and after 50 metres you will arrive at the **Aga Khan Shia Imami Ismaili**. This stately looking four-storey building was built in honour of Aga Khan III, the spiritual leader of the Shia Imami Ismaili Muslims till 1957 (the current leader is his son, Aga Khan IV). The four-bay building dates from the nineteenth century and is detailed with particularly fine metal balconies and plaster motifs in creamy white and yellow colours. Each floor has four full-length French windows set in arched alcoves.

8 Kalupur Darwaza

Follow the road for 200 metres and take a left and you will see another city gate, the Kalupur Darwaza. Ahmedabad's city wall not

not only protected the city from military threats, it also indirectly led to the formation of a local government. During the nineteenth century the city walls had decayed because of floods and lack of maintenance. To address this problem the Town Wall Fund Committee was set up in 1831. Although initially focusing on the city wall, in the following decades the committee extended its functions to the levying of local taxes, the maintenance of roads, installation of street lighting, and implementation of drainage schemes. The committee was transformed into the Ahmedabad municipality in 1885. As the city expanded rapidly in the twentieth century there was pressure to demolish the city walls, despite the cultural significance of the structure and the cost of demolition. Sadly, the city walls were gradually dismantled and today only some pieces survive here and there.

9 Manamiya Hava Tower

Pass under the Kalupur Darwaza city gate and keep walking down Tankshal Road for about 350 metres. Looming in front of you will be the Manamiya Hava Tower. This was built as a clock tower overlooking the market area in 1925. The buttresses on each corner are painted a shade of greenish blue and each of its four storeys is slightly different, featuring different kinds of medallions, windows and balustrades. Facing the market across the road stands the **Sakar Khan Masjid**. This mosque does not quite measure up to the architectural quality of some of the other medieval structures in the city. Built during the reign of Mahmud Begada in the second half of the fifteenth century, it is single storey and does not sport any minarets neither does it have a proper facade.

Link to Kalupur Walk:
Follow Tankshal Road for another 600 metres.

Kalupur

Kalupur was the area of the city originally occupied by the Hindu and Jain communities. Other neighbourhoods in the old city were usually connected to a Muslim nobleman and each had its own court and maintained a local mosque. Ahmed Shah realized that in order to make his city prosper he had to welcome other communities into the city too. Shah invited local Jain and Hindu communities to settle in the city and also allowed them to establish temples. It is surprising that the area he decided to be suitable was right next to the Jama Masjid, the Muslim centre of prayer. This part of the city still has an intense mix of commerce, temples and housing communities which give it its appeal. The historic and contemporary significance of the area also led the municipality to start a heritage walk here in 1997.

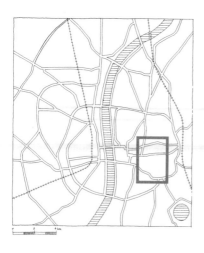

Key

1. Tankshal ni Haveli
2. Mahaveerswami Derasar
3. Old Central Bank
4. Fernandes Bridge
5. Harkunvar Shethani ni Haveli
6. Ashtapad Derasar
7. Jagvallah Derasar
8. Shantinath Derasar
9. Kala Ramji Mandir
10. Kavi Dalpatram Chowk
11. Swaminarayan Mandir

Walk 5

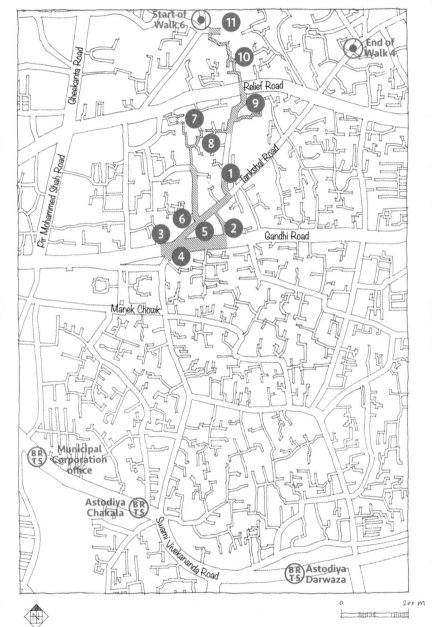

1 Tankshal ni Haveli

About halfway down Tankshal Road a wide *pol* branches off the main road. Enter it and after 40 metres you will see the enormous wooden facade of the Tankshal ni Haveli on your right. This three-storey *haveli* has the longest wooden facade in the old city, measuring 25 metres. It has a classic three-tiered system, typical for Ahmedabad. The

ground floor has a raised *otla*, upon which a series of columns with carved brackets support the main living quarters on the first floor. This floor contains more elaborate carvings, featuring floral motifs and large windows to allow in breeze. The top floor is executed in a much plainer manner. The *haveli* was probably constructed in the nineteenth century and takes its name from the coin-minting activities that used to take place in this part of the city (*tankshal* means 'mint'). In 1925 the *haveli* came into the possession of the Ahmedabad municipality and part of it was used as a girls' school. Unfortunately, there were no funds available for its maintenance and it has been abandoned for over 25 years. The City Heritage Centre is currently restoring it to its former glory.

2 Mahaveerswami Derasar

Opening times: daily, 6am to 1pm, 3.15 to 9pm
Admission: free

Head back to Tankshal Road and follow it for 80 metres. Take a left and follow the lane as it gently slopes upwards towards Gandhi Road, then take a right and almost immediately you will see the Mahaveerswami Derasar facing onto Gandhi Road. This Jain temple dates from 1864 and is typical for this religion's tradition in its main entrance adorned by marble *torana*s or archways artistically carved with dancers who seem to welcome the believers with music. As in most Jain temples, the use of electricity is not condoned and oil lamps are used to light the interior. In this case the interior is completely covered in marble. There is a passage behind the main idol. This temple is part of the Shwetambar sect of Jainism, an influential sect which takes its name from the term 'white-clad', referring to the robes worn by the sect's monks. (Did you know? The temple mountain of Palitana in Gujarat is the most holy place for Jains.)

3 Old Central Bank

Continue walking along Gandhi Road for about 180 metres until you see the Old Central Bank on your right. The main structure of this four-storey building is made up of alternating bands of red brick and beige sandstone. In between these are bay windows with small iron balconies. The bank was constructed in 1923—but it is the Gujarati date that is used on the building's facade, following the Vikram Samvat calendar (which is 56.7 years ahead of the Christian one). This was the head office of the State Bank of India but in 1957 there was an armed robbery and the bank decided to move to another location where a new head office was designed by B.V. Doshi and opened in Lal Darwaza in 1966. Two buildings to the left of the bank, the **Dudhai Apartment** building, are from the same era. Dating from 1933, it is a beautiful blend of architectural styles with the top floors feeling more modern with their carved rounded balustrades and extensive use of glass. The base of the building although detailed in a neoclassical style has the window arches detailed in

gothic style; it also has a lot of highly decorative plasterwork. The ground floor is double height and provides spaces for shops.

4 Fernandes Bridge

Leave Gandhi Road by taking the stairs down to Tankshal Road; at this junction Tankshal Road lies several metres below Gandhi Road. The reason for this is that Tankshal Road used to be a creek and would have been a natural route to the Jama Masijd and the Bhadra complex before the city walls were built in 1487. Nowadays Tankshal Road is completely urbanized and connects to Kalupur Darwaza at the edge of the old walled city. Fernandes Bridge was constructed by the British administrators across this dried-up creek in 1884 and named after the engineer who built it. There is an educational books market underneath the bridge where you can also see some of its old foundations.

5 Harkunvar Shethani ni Haveli

Follow Tankshal Road in a north-easterly direction for about 100 metres and you will see the huge Harkunvar Shethani ni Haveli on your right-hand side. This townhouse has 60 rooms and belongs to the wealthy Jain merchant family of Hutheesing. This family has a prosperous history in this city. They moved to the region around 250 years ago from Osian in Rajasthan. They were aware of the declining trade across the Mughal Empire and were orienting themselves to the increasing commerce from across the sea. They first settled in Cambay, and then started building up their trading network in Ahmedabad. Hutheesing was actually the first name of the man who moved here and the family adopted it as their family name thereafter. This family is perhaps best known for the Hutheesing Temple they built north of the walled city (see the Mirzapur Road Walk). The towering *haveli* here actually has only three stories, but each is almost double-height. Part of the ground floor has ionic columns, while the other side of the ground floor facade has some of the largest wooden brackets in the city, some of which even feature elephants. The upper floors have a mix of iron and woodwork. The *haveli* is not open to public.

6 Ashtapad Derasar

Opening times: daily, 6am to 12noon, 5 to 6pm
Admission: free

Directly adjacent to the Harkunvar Shethani ni Haveli, on the opposite side of Tankshal Road, is the Ashtapad Derasar. The outer facade of this Jain temple has the appearance of a two-storey *haveli*. The top floor has four *jharoka*s and is decorated with dancers and musicians in a style typical of Jain temples. The entry doorway leads to a staircase that opens into a courtyard where the free-standing marble temple is located. Viewed from the entrance the plan is a linear arrangement of the entrance pavilion, the temple, then a second pavilion and the *nandeshwar deep*. The *nandeshwar deep* can be recognized by the towering *shikhara*. The temple has a roof featuring many small indentations. The entire complex was built in 1856 by Sheth Maganlal Karamchand. Next door is a Jain school and a shop. This historic building acts as a temporary residence for Jain monks and their apprentices. There is a temple and large assembly hall on the first floor. Upon exiting the temple take a left. This *pol* is called **Doshiwada ni Pol** and is known for its community of goldsmiths. There are many jewellery shops along this stretch of the road, as well as many traditional *haveli*s. There is also an ornamental bird-feeder with distinctly colonial influences. Keep following the winding road for about 250 metres until you arrive at **Simandhar Swami ni Khadaki**. This well-preserved *pol* has some beautiful *haveli*s.

7 Jagvallah Derasar

Opening times: daily, 6am to 12noon, 4pm to 6pm
Admission: free

From Simandhar Swami ni Khadaki it is possible to see Jagvallah Derasar. To reach it, leave the *pol* at the northern side and walk around the block—keep turning right until you get to it. At first, this temple seems to have two entrances. One entrance is made of wood and deliberately looks like a *haveli*; the actual entrance is of marble and is off to the side. This arrangement might have come about because several idols from Saraspur were relocated to this Jain temple in the eighteenth century to save them from destruction. The story goes that the 700-year-old idol of *tirthankara*s was too big to be placed inside the old temple, so a new entrance had to be made. It was probably placed below ground to safeguard it from future raids.

The temple interior consists of two levels interconnected by an open space in the centre with staircases on either side. The entire building is made from white marble, including the dome which contains a central lotus flower and 18 sculptures of dancing girls. Throughout the temple one can access the backyard, which contains another shrine as well as an underground water tank. From here it is also possible to see the decorative patterns on the temple exterior. One motif is the *dharmachakra* (or the Wheel of the Law), seen here flanked by two game animals (usually black buck deer), this symbolizes the last sermon of the Jains. A similar concept is found in Buddhism where this symbol represents Buddha's first lessons, which were taught to his disciples in a game park. The complex is thought to be around 400 years old, although parts of the building might have been refurbished and added later.

8 Shantinath Derasar

Opening times: daily, 6am to 11am, 5pm to 6pm
Admission: free

Retrace your steps to Simandhar Swami ni Khadaki and take a left inside the alley towards **Shantinath Pol**. This well-preserved *pol* contains various heritage *haveli*s, several Jain temples and a *chabutara* as well. The most significant structure in it is the **Shantinath Derasar**, which is located at the back of the *pol*. This modest looking marble temple stands on a plinth, the front part of which functions as an *otla*. The *otla* has five bays of columns connected by *torana*s and is decorated with sculptures of dancing girls. The temple's origins are thought to be around 425 years old but it was heavily renovated at the start of the twentieth century. The original structure was entirely made out of wood and parts of this old wooden structure can still be seen on the inside. The dark polished wood ceiling is a unique feature, as are the wooden statues. The layout of the temple is typical, with an octagonal supporting structure for the dome and a passage behind the main idol.

9 Kala Ramji Mandir

Opening times: daily, dawn to dusk
Admission: free

Leave Shantinath Pol and take a left, then immediately take a right and enter Haja Patel ni Pol. At the back of the *pol*, on your left-hand side, you will find the **Kala Ramji Mandir**. This building is a unique combination of residential dwelling and sacred shrine. The L-shaped exterior facade that is visible from the street has a high ground-floor with beautifully carved columns and brackets. You enter the house via the door on the right. Continue walking to the left until you arrive at a courtyard, which is at the centre of the building. The carved woodwork that is now painted in a grey-green colour was originally painted in more vibrant tones. The fluted columns hold brackets that are carved with musicians and dancers, very unlike the more usual flower patterns. The frieze above the columns has images of animals, such as peacocks and monkeys. At the back of the courtyard is the main shrine of the temple which holds a sitting black marble statue of Lord Ram, an avatar of the Hindu god Vishnu and best known as the hero of the epic Ramayana. In this story, Sita, the wife of Ram, is abducted by evil king Ravan and the tale tells how Ram, with the help of the monkey god Hanuman, wages war against Ravan and manages to rescue Sita. Ram and Sita return to their capital at Ayodhya and subsequently start to rule over an age of peace, harmony and prosperity known as the Ram Rajya and which was supposed to have lasted for 11,000 years.

The entire house currently has around 80 residents, some of whom represent the eighteenth generation since the foundation of the temple and who have been taking care of the building all this time. The building is thought to be around 350 years old. Despite the residents' good work, funding has become a problem and until recently the building was in bad condition. Fortunately conservation work was recently carried out by an international team of architects.

⑩ Kavi Dalpatram Chowk

Retrace your steps towards the main lane and take a right and you will come to Relief Road. Until recently the Calico dome used to stand here, but had to be dismantled due to poor maintenance. The concrete dome had been designed by Gautam Sarabhai and used to be the venue for such events as Ahmedabad's first ever fashion show. The memory of the dome is interlinked with another famous architect, Frank Lloyd Wright, who was initially commissioned to design an office building here but plans fell through. Go across Relief Road and head inside the **Lambeshwar ni Pol** directly opposite. Continue until you reach **Kavi Dalpatram Chowk**. Dalpatram was a Gujarati poet who lived from 1820 to 1898. At the age of 24 he came to Ahmedabad to study Sanskrit at the nearby Swaminarayan temple. The building that you see behind the *chowk* is actually only a replica facade. His actual house, which used to stand on this site, is now the open space of the *chowk*.

⑪ Swaminarayan Mandir

Opening times: Daily, dawn to dusk
Phone: +91 98 2403 2866
(heritage walk)

From Kavi Dalpatram Chowk you can see the roof of the Swaminarayan Mandir directly to the north. Follow the *pol* in a northerly direction to find its main entrance. First you will come across the **Swaminarayan Dharmashala**. Take a right and you will see the impressive main gate of the Swaminarayan temple.

Built here in 1822, this was the first Swaminarayan temple in the world. The followers of this Hindu sect believe in the teachings of Swaminarayan, who lived from 1781 to 1830 (five other temples were built during his lifetime). Swaminarayan was born as Ghanshyam Pande in Uttar Pradesh. He lost his parents at the age of 11 after which he set off on a pilgrimage that lasted seven years. He eventually settled with an existing sect in Gujarat, where he duly became leader at the tender age of 21. Swaminarayan was extremely devoted to the ancient Hindu scriptures and believed that he was an incarnation of the god Krishna. The Swaminarayan faith currently has around 20 million followers, many of them residing in Gujarat.

The *mandir* or temple was made possible by a land grant by the British, with whom Swaminarayan maintained a good relationship. It has a large *mandapa* adorned with *torana*s and dancing girls. There are three *shikhara*s containing idols of Radha, Krishna, Nar and Narayan and, to the right, Swaminarayan and his parents. The temple stands inside a large courtyard surrounded by a three-storey U-shaped building that contains residences, guest houses and audience halls. This complex was added to the temple in 1871 and constructed using teak painted white, which highlights the vibrant colours of the brackets and arches making up the arcades. Since there is strict segregation of men and women within the sect, the quarters of both are separated. The quarters for women are adjacent to the main entrance and the ladies who live here have taken vows of celibacy and devote their life to the temple. The three-storey courtyard is painted white, with accents in brown. The arcades run around the entire courtyard giving it a sense of calm which is very different from its outer facade. The main audience hall faces the temple and provides access to the male quarters. Behind the audience hall, on the right, there is a small two-storey wooden pavilion which still has some of its original mural paintings and mosaics. Before leaving the complex make sure to view the opulent entrance gate. This is in a baroque style, with many colours and architectural elements and iconography from the Hindu tradition as well as the Marathi and Rajasthani folk cultures. It also contains some European elements, such as the Corinthian capitals.

The residences themselves are in a gothic style, reminiscent of Gujarat College built in 1887.

Note: The Ahmedabad municipality organizes a daily heritage walk that roughly follows the walk described in this chapter. It starts at the Swaminarayan temple at 8 pm and takes about two-and-a-half hours. Participation fee is Rs. 100 for non-Indians.

Link to Mirzapur Road Walk:
Leave the Swaminarayan temple and take a right then follow the main lane for 400 metres.

Mirzapur Road

Nearest BRTS: Delhi Darwaza
Walking time: 2 hours and
30 minutes

The Mirzapur area lies just north of the central Bhadra area in the old city, wedged between Shahpur to the west and Dariyapur to the east. The neighbourhood straddles Mirzapur and Gheekanta roads which join just before passing through Delhi Darwaza. Historically both of these roads were the main trading routes from Ahmedabad to Delhi. Perhaps for that reason there are many large Sultanate-era mosques, which would have been visible to any visitors coming into the city. They show a great variety of styles and reflect the plurality of the city. After the British came, large chunks of land were made available for several large new Christian schools. This walk also extends towards the Hutheesing Temple, one of the main architectural icons of the city.

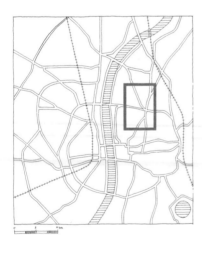

Key

1 Jadabhagat ni Pol

2 Tadkeshwar Mandir

3 Muhafiz Khan Masjid

4 St. Xavier's High School

5 Rani Rupmati Masjid

6 Ranchhodlal Chhotalal Girls High School

7 Conflictorium

8 Sultan Qutbuddin Masjid

9 Achratlal Girdharlal Tower

10 Fateh Masjid

11 Hutheesing Temple

Walk 6

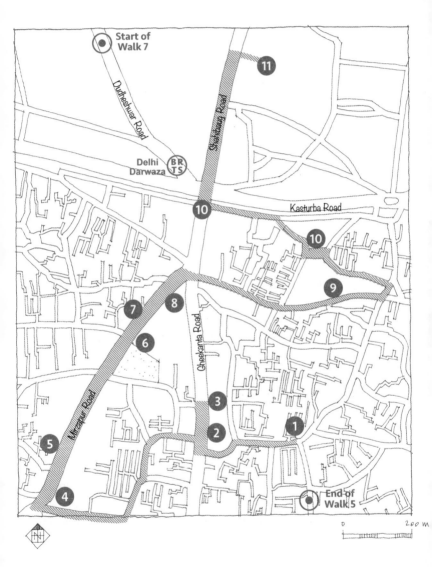

1 Jadabhagat ni Pol

Jadabhagat ni Pol is one of the best preserved clusters of *pol* houses in the old city. In this one you get a sense of what an original *pol* must have looked like several hundred years ago. It is essentially an L-shaped layout, from which several smaller lanes are accessible. The largest houses are along the main *pol*, while the secondary alleys contain smaller homes. In total about 70 families live here. Most houses in Jadabhagat ni Pol are occupied by members of the Patel caste. The *haveli*s were built without the employment of an architect. A *haveli*'s plan was based on an assessment of the needs of the household and site conditions. A rough plan was made to show the arrangement of the various rooms, but other drawings, like elevations, sections or details were not drawn. The best preserved houses in this *pol* are a series of four **green-painted three-storey havelis** along the main *pol*. They all have a similar structure, and are typical for *haveli*s in Ahmedabad. The ground floor is raised a few steps, and has an *otla* just in front of the main door. The first floor has large full-height windows that can open to give the residents a view of the street and allow for breeze to flow into the interior. The second floor extends further out over the street supported by carved brackets.

2 Tadkeshwar Mandir

Opening times: daily, dawn to dusk
Admission: free

Leave Jadabhagat ni Pol and head right. After 150 metres there is a Y-shaped junction where you should keep to the left. Once you reach Gheekanta Road take a right. The Tadkeshwar Mandir is situated directly on the right behind a row of shops. Pass through the entry passage and you will face the side elevation of this whitewashed and moss-covered temple. Dedicated to Lord Shiva, this temple was founded around 200 years ago by the rulers of the Maratha Empire, rulers of Ahmedabad at the time. Its layout is typical for Nagara-style temples.

The domed *mandapa*, or entrance vestibule, has three protruding porches that are also domed and are decorated with sculptures of dancers with ceremonial serpentine-shaped *torana*s connecting the columns. Unfortunately, the spaces between the columns have been filled in over time. The edge of the roof has several figures, including elephants and lions. A special feature of this temple is its two *chhatri*s on the *shikhara* facing the main entrance and the *jharoka*s protruding out of the *shikhara*. Inside can be seen Nandi, the vehicle of Shiva, and *lingam*, two elements to be found in all Shiva temples.

③ Muhafiz Khan Masjid

Opening times: daily, dawn to dusk (closed during prayers)
Admission: free

Just 50 metres north of Tadkeshwar Mandir stands the Muhafiz Khan Masjid. This small mosque represents yet another architectural experiment under the reign of Mahmud Begada. It faces west towards Mecca and thus has its back to the road. From the road it is clearly visible that the mosque has a lower rear, with three domes, and a higher front facade. Both its minarets are still intact. The prayer hall is compact, without any wings extending beyond the position of the minarets. The building has three high-arched entrance doors, with three small ornamental *jharoka*s above them. The side elevation of the building has two full-sized carved *jharoka*s. The *qibla* wall has a beautifully carved *mihrab* of marble. The mosque was built by Jamal ud-din Silahdar in 1485; he later received the title Muhafiz Khan and was a nobleman at the Sultanate court. According to literature he was successful in his tasks as an administrator, especially in repressing crime. His simple open-pillared tomb stands in the mosque's grounds.

④ St. Xavier's High School

Head back south along Gheekanta Road for 200 metres. Then take a right and after 150 metres head left. At the next junction take a right again and continue for 200 metres till you reach Mirzapur Road. On the corner is the compound of the St. Xavier's High School. This school was established in 1935 by the Mount Carmel sisters. It was soon taken over by the Jesuits, who expanded it to its present form. Until 2007, it functioned as a boys' high school, teaching in English as well as Gujarati. Since that date girls have also been allowed to attend. The grounds are very peaceful and the buildings are arranged around an open courtyard. The main building (on your right) is clad in yellow sandstone and has three storeys and a large central porch supporting a tower. The windows are framed by white Ionic columns.

The classrooms are arranged along arcades on either side of the central tower. At the back of the compound stands a church that was built in 1970 (on the site of an old one). Its unorthodox design lets light in from the triangular spaces underneath the roof in what is otherwise a plain and simple interior. The original church was built in 1842 and was the oldest in Ahmedabad before it was demolished.

5 Rani Rupmati Masjid

Opening times: daily, dawn to dusk (closed during prayers)
Admission: free

Just a little bit beyond the St. Xavier's High School, across the road, stands the Rani Rupmati Masjid. The mosque was probably built in the early decades of the sixteenth century under the reign of Muzaffar Shah. The Rani Rupmati Masjid has many features that are characteristic of Gujarat Sultanate architecture. The facade is dominated by two large carved buttresses that would have originally supported minarets, both of which have collapsed. The central part of the mosque is raised one storey above the rest of the building and the central arched doorway is positioned within a rectangular frame, with lotus medallions on its corners. The lower parts of the front facade of the prayer hall have smaller arches and two *jharoka*s on either side. There is a dome positioned behind each entrance, supported by an octagonal structure of columns. The entire building is made from sandstone, except the *mihrab*, which is carved from marble. This mosque also has a domed *rauda*, which contains two tombs.

6 Ranchhodlal Chhotalal Girls High School

Christ Church Mirzapur
Opening times: daily, dawn to dusk
Admission: free

Continue to walk along Mirzapur Road for around 500 metres, where, behind a row of trees opening up onto a large plot of land, you will see **Christ Church Mirzapur**. This simple cream-coloured place of worship

was built by the Church of North India. From the church it is possible to see the south facade of the school building which dates from 1916, which is when the high school opened. Largely funded by Ranchhodlal Chhotalal, who had made his considerable wealth from the cotton industry, the red-brick building is organized symmetrically around a central entrance, with two small domed towers emulating medieval battlements. The rear of the central part of the building echoes the octagonal shape of the chapel. On opposite ends of the building are two more domed structures. The classrooms open onto the arcades on either side of the building.

7 Conflictorium

Opening times: Tuesday to Sunday, 11am to 8pm
Admission: free
www.conflictorium@gmail.com
+91-79-2562 0747

Directly opposite the Ranchhodlal Chhotalal Girls High School stands the Conflictorium, which is a participatory museum, meaning that it is based not around artefacts but rather on experiences and on building consciousness. India generally, and Ahmedabad specifically, has had a history of communal violence, but also of great social and emancipatory achievements. The museum explores some of these facets through workshops, performances and art installations. Situated in a historic two-storey building dating from the early twentieth century, the Gool Lodge, as it was known, was owned by a Parsi family who operated a beauty salon in it. The last remaining member of the family, Bachuben Nagarwala, was the first professionally trained hair-stylist in the city and when she died she donated the house so that it could be converted into a museum. Part of the first floor is still occupied by the family who rented out the donated part of the house. The building is constructed in a Western neoclassical style, with simple stucco decoration and a quirky pointed roof. The first floor still has its original stained-glass windows.

8 Sultan Qutbuddin Masjid

Opening times: daily, dawn to dusk (closed during prayers)
Admission: free

Diagonally across from the Conflictorium stands the Sultan Qutbuddin Masjid which has its entrance on the north side. The mosque was built around 1449, even before the city walls were constructed, and is located on the road that leads from the heart of the old city to Delhi. It is likely that this would have been the first building that visitors could see when arriving from Delhi. The overall form is much like the oldest mosque in Ahmedabad, the Ahmed Shah Masjid in Bhadra. There is one central arch which has two adjoining buttresses and two smaller arches on either side of these. The minarets are lost but the buttresses of the mosque remain and are much larger and more intricately decorated than the Ahmed Shah Masjid. The arches are decorated with lotus medallions. The central dome inside the mosque is one storey higher than the rest of the building and is supported by eight unusually shaped columns—they take the form of eight-pointed stars. An Arabic inscription on the *mihrab* ascribes the construction to a Nizam, a keeper of the arsenal during the rule of Qutbuddin Ahmed Shah II.

9 Achratlal Girdharlal Tower

After leaving the mosque, head to the junction of Mirzapur and Gheekanta roads and take a right. Follow the street for 400 metres till you reach the five-storey clock tower of the Achratlal Girdharlal Trust. Achratlal was a wealthy business man who decided to donate funds for the construction of a hostel for students. When it was built in 1884, it was one of the few places where students from villages could stay while studying in Ahmedabad. The hostel is organized around a pleasant courtyard, filled with creepers and palm trees. A wide veranda runs around the courtyard giving access to the student rooms. The facade facing the street has a long *otla* on which a row of neoclassical stone columns support the second floor. The clock tower starts from the first floor, breaking the structure of arches and the oval-shaped parapet.

10 Fateh Masjid

Opening times: daily, 1:30pm to 6pm (closed during prayers)
Admission: free

Head east for another 100 metres to arrive at a busy *chowk*; take two left turns and follow the lane for 200 metres. The entrance to the

Fateh Masjid is marked by two newly-added minarets. This mosque is likely to have been built by Darya Khan, a nobleman at the court of Mahmud Begada, who also gave his name to the area. The mosque has a simple open facade, with five domes. During construction, one of the domes developed a crack leading the locals to call the mosque 'Phuti Masjid' (cracked mosque) instead of Fateh Masjid (victory mosque). Upon leaving the mosque take a right and follow the lane for 300 metres. You are walking along the alignment of where the city wall used to be, which becomes apparent once you reach the Delhi Darwaza city gate. Delhi Darwaza is one of the biggest gates to survive in the city. Most city gates had only one entrance, but this was the gate that connected to the main road to Delhi and has additional, smaller gates on either side. The arches sport lotus medallions. The use of the lotus flower as a decorative motif has a long tradition in Indian architecture, dating back at least 2,000 years to early rock carvings. In earlier Hindu, Jain and Buddhist architecture the lotus was often used as a pedestal for a deity because it was seen as representing pure form. Under Islamic rule the flowers tended to be represented in isolation.

11 Hutheesing Temple

Opening times: daily, dawn to dusk (closed during prayers)
Admission: free (photography not allowed)

To reach the Hutheesing Temple, go through the city gate and follow Shahibaug Road in a northerly direction for 350 metres. The first building you will notice is the large ornamental tower called **Maanstambha**. This was only built in 2002 and it is a replica of a similar tower in the majestic fort complex of Chittorgarh in Rajasthan. Maanstambha, meaning the column of honour, was built to celebrate the 2,500th anniversary of the birth of Mahavira, the twenty-fourth, and last, *tirthankar*, or 'crossing maker', who is accredited with establishing the principals of Jainism.

The Hutheesing Temple stands on a slight setback from the main road and was constructed in 1848 by architect Premchand Salat.

It is the biggest Jain temple in the city. Its site was originally the residence of the Hutheesing family. Their compound, which housed their extended family, featured temples, gardens and guesthouses. Sheth Hutheesing wanted to build a temple on the complex, possibly to provide employment during a severe famine in Gujarat. The merchant, however, died at the age of 49 and was only able to lay the foundation stone. The construction was then supervised by his wife, Shethani Harkunvar. The building is entered by ascending some steps underneath a gateway pavilion. The entrance has the appearance of a traditional *haveli* but instead of wood is built completely of marble. Domestic architectural elements, like *jharoka*s and *chhajja*s, can be seen on the first floor. The entire pavilion is richly carved with musicians and dancers who welcome devotees. A strange element can be found at the bottom of the steps, where a small Hindu shrine devoted to Shiva can be found. Once inside the complex the layout is that of a traditional temple, with the main building positioned in the centre and surrounded by a colonnade. This colonnade is home to an additional 52 shrines, or *devakulika*s, each one topped by a *shikhara*. The *shikhara*s are constructed of brick with a plaster render. The main two-storey building is essentially a sequence of three spaces. First, one ascends the elevated domed pavilion or *mandapa*, decorated with arched *torana*s and sculptures of dancers and musicians. One arm of its cross-shaped plan leads to the main double-height hall. To the rear is located the main sanctum containing five deities. There is also an underground cellar containing a number of other deities and holding a flame that has been burning continually since 1848.

Link to Shahibaug Walk:
Head back to Delhi Darwaza, take a right and follow Dudheshwar Road for one kilometre.

Shahibaug

Nearest BRTS: Gurudwara BRTS
Walking time: 3 hours

The area wedged in-between the northern part of the walled city and the Sabarmati River is called Shahibaug, which literally means Royal Garden and refers to the principal building of the area: the Moti Shahi Palace built under the reign of Mughal Emperor Shah Jahan in 1622. The old city was and still is crowded and this area provided space for those with money to build spacious homes and lush gardens. The wealthy and powerful of Ahmedabad naturally felt inclined to build their own houses in close proximity to the palace. When the British came they also chose this area for the establishment of their cantonment. This part of the city still retains some of this old-world atmosphere, with large shady trees lining the wide avenues. (This walk also includes two buildings that are located across the river.)

Key

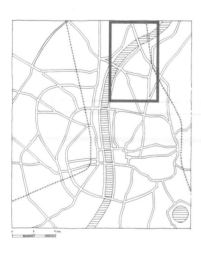

1. Bibi Achut Kuki Masjid
2. Darya Khan's Tomb
3. Masonic Lodge
4. Calico Museum of Textiles
5. Sardar Patel National Memorial
6. Circuit House
7. Khan Chishti Masjid
8. Chinubhai Baronet House
9. Gandhi Ashram
10. Manav Sadhna Campus

Walk 7

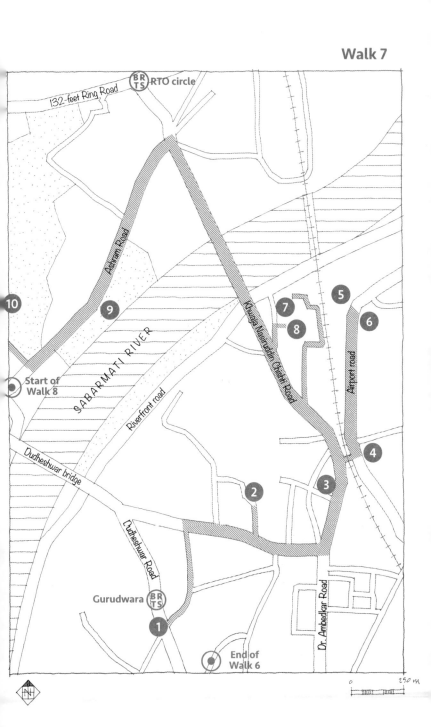

RTO circle

132-feet Ring Road

Ashram Road

10

9

SABARMATI RIVER

Khwaja Nasiruddin Chishti Road

7

5

8

6

Airport road

Riverfront road

Start of
Walk 8

Dudheshwar bridge

4

2

3

Dudheshwar Road

Gurudwara

1

Dr. Ambedkar Road

End of
Walk 6

0   250 m

1 Bibi Achut Kuki Masjid

Opening times: Daily, dawn to dusk
Admission: free

From the Gurudwara BRTS station head to the western side of the road and look out for the metal entrance gate; this has Shahi Masjid inscribed on it in Gujarati. The small alley opens into grounds from where you can enter the enclosure of the Bibi Achut Kuki Masjid. This mosque was built during the reign of Mahmud Begada in 1469 by a local nobleman about whom almost nothing is known. The reign of Begada is known for its architectural experimentation, and in this case led to a fine blend of Hindu and Islamic styles executed in sandstone—for example, the door threshold at the entrance gate is shaped like those

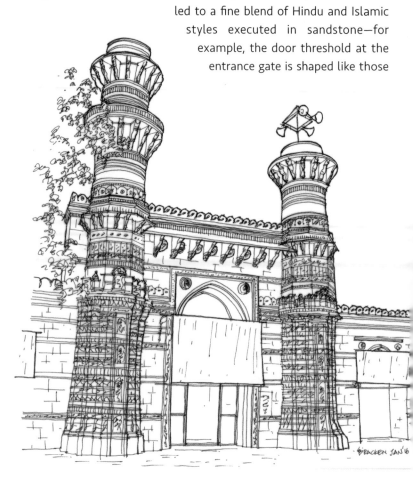

in Hindu or Jain temples. The mosque has an unusually large enclosure, which means that it possibly originally contained a garden. This seven-bay place of worship is similar in style to the Kutub Shah Masjid built in nearby Mirzapur about 20 years earlier. Here, however, the minarets are largely still intact and there is an elegant canopy connecting them. The central dome is carved with concentric petal motifs and raised as a storey above the rest of the structure. The nearby tomb has been crudely amalgamated into a more recent concrete structure.

2 Darya Khan's Tomb

Opening times: Daily, dawn to dusk
Admission: free

From the main road take the lane opposite Bibi Achut Kuki Masjid and follow it until you come to another main road where you should take a right. After about 200 metres take a left and you will see the enormous whitewashed dome of Darya Khan's Tomb at the end of the approach lane. This is not only the largest tomb in Ahmedabad, measuring almost 40 square metres; it is also the only entirely brick-built tomb in the city. Darya Khan was a nobleman who had settled in the court of Ahmed Shah. The area where he lived is now called Dariyapur, in the northern part of the walled city. The architecture of the tomb, with the sort of brick arches more usually associated with Persian architecture and the fact that its early construction date of 1453 has led some to speculate that Darya Khan or his architect had some connection with Persia; one that he wished to immortalize in architecture. The tomb has nothing of the fine delicate carving that is characteristic of other Islamic buildings in Ahmedabad and instead relies on brick squinches and niches to mark the transition from brick pillars to the dome. The central chamber is surrounded by a wide circular corridor that is presently used as a place for rope making. A large drum to be found in the central chamber is used every day while prayers are being said before the grave of Darya Khan.

③ Masonic Lodge

Head back to the main road and take a left till you come to a large T-junction. Take a left towards the Shahibaug underpass and continue walking for about 200 metres. On your left-hand side you should find the Masonic Lodge of Fellowship of Salem. With the coming of the British, Freemasonry was also introduced to India. The first lodge in the country was established in Calcutta in 1730. Initially, Masonic lodges in India were for the British only but as early as 1812 the first Indians were allowed to enter this secret society. Many prominent Indians were Freemasons, for example Motilal Nehru, father of the first Prime Minister Jawaharlal Nehru. Across India there are 320 Masonic lodges and more than 22,000 members. The lodge in Ahmedabad was established in 1908, under the constitution of the Scottish Grand Lodge. It is a simple building with a wooden roof, in a style similar to that of other buildings from that period such as the Gujarat College. When a Grand Lodge was opened in New Delhi in 1961, the lodge in Ahmedabad joined it, leaving the Scottish Lodge. Continue walking towards Shahibaug underpass, under the railway tracks, and you will pass an equestrian **statue of Maharana Pratap**. He is best known for his stance against the Mughals in the Battle of Haldighati at Chittorgarh in 1576.

④ Calico Museum of Textiles

Opening times: Daily (closed on Wednesday)
Admission: free (by appointment only)
Havelis: *Begins at 10.15am*
Admission: free (by appointment only)
Museum: *Begins at 2.45pm*
Admission: free (by appointment only)

www.calicomuseum.org
+91 99 79738650

Pass underneath the railway tracks via the Shahibaug underpass. Continue up the ramp on the left-hand side and turn immediately to the right upon reaching the road level and you will come to the Calico Museum of Textiles which has one of the most impressive collections of textiles in India. Moreover, the museum is housed in one of the most delightful architectural gems in Ahmedabad. The main building was designed by the architect Surendranath in 1930 as a residence for the Sarabhai family. Set in a lush semi-tropical garden full of peacocks and monkeys, it makes the whole compound seem like one of the mythical scenes about Krishna depicted on the woven textiles on display inside. The museum was founded when the Sarabhai family and the Calico Textile Mill decided to make a place to preserve and promote the traditional textiles of India. The museum opened its door in 1949, initially at another location. It was only in 1983, when the Calico Textile Mills were no longer able to provide funds for the museum, that it shifted to its present location. The museum is now managed by the Sarabhai Foundation and is divided into two parts that can be visited by pre-arranged guided walks.

This **first guided walk** takes you inside the *haveli*s around the *chowk*. The *chowk* was previously used as a swimming-pool complex and when the building was converted into a museum wooden facades from demolished buildings in the old city were re-used in its construction. The three *haveli*s all have finely carved wooden panels and brackets. Each room is dedicated to textiles from a different region. One starts with block-printed textiles from Andhra Pradesh, the second contains silk saris from the Maratha Empire. There are also Pashmina textiles from Kashmir and dolls from Rajasthan. Of course there are also several examples of Gujarati textiles. One unique item in the collection is a large wooden cart from Chennai used to carry an idol of Shiva. The final part of the tour takes you back to the main building where there are texts and images explaining the production techniques of the various different textiles.

The **second guided walk** takes you through most of the main building. The first room has a collection of statues of gods, including Shiva and

Krishna, in various materials. You then go outside through part of the garden towards the temple. Like the buildings around the *chowk*, the temple and other parts of the building incorporate wooden elements from old *haveli*s that were rescued when their houses were being demolished. From the temple you go to the main staircase which is decorated with carved wooden panels of Indian teak and which has a marble floor. The white marble comes from Italy, while the other colours were quarried in Rajasthan. The central part of the exhibition is the collection of *pichhavai*s, or large hand-woven and hand-painted cotton textiles. These textiles were used in temples across Rajasthan to tell stories about Krishna. The top floor has a series of miniature paintings and South Indian bronze statues. What is most special here, though, is the use of traditional wooden elements like the numerous elephant brackets that are unlike anything to be seen in the old city. It is also possible to see the brightly coloured mosaics on the roof of the ground floor below, which features a tree and lotus flowers.

⑤ Sardar Patel National Memorial

Opening times: Daily, 9.30am to 5.30pm (closed on Monday)
Admission charges apply
www.sardarpatelmuseum.org

Upon leaving the Calico Museum of Textiles follow Airport Road northwards for about 600 metres. This road leads you past several nice-looking bungalows. At the far end of its tree-lined length, where the road bends to the right, sits the Moti Shahi Mahal, home to the Sardar Patel National Memorial. This palace was built in 1622, during Mughal rule, by the Viceroy of Ahmedabad, Shah Jahan. Shah Jahan was not yet emperor—he would become so in 1628, during which time he would commission other notable buildings, such as the world-famous Taj Mahal in Agra. The Shahi Mahal is considerably more modest but still an interesting place to see, especially since it is one of the few buildings dating back to Mughal times still standing in Ahmedabad. The palace stands three-storeys tall on a broad plinth, crowned with octagonal pavilions on each corner. A double-height entrance in a Persian style gives access to a symmetrical plan that actually strongly resembles the layout of a Mughal tomb. The building was commissioned to provide employment during a famine. Originally it also had a large garden, but sadly not much of this is left. When the British came to control the city they occupied the building and used it for government functions such as the residence of a judge. It was in that role that the building became home to the famous poet and philosopher Rabindranath Tagore (for six months in 1878). His brother was working at the law courts and Tagore, who was only 17, stayed in the palace to study English before leaving to study law in England. After Independence, the building was home of the Governor of Gujarat before becoming the Sardar Patel National Memorial in 1980. Sardar Patel was one of the emblematic figures in India's freedom struggle as well as the first Home Minister of Independent India. He had received his legal training in Britain and first worked for

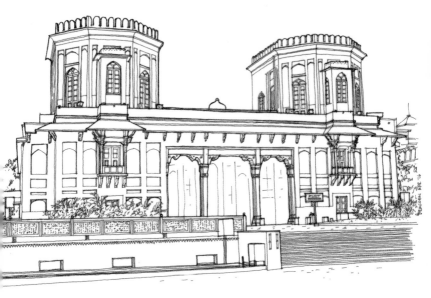

the municipal authorities in Ahmedabad. In 1928 things changed, he became the leader of the Bardoli Satyagraha, an act of civil obedience against government taxes. He burned his Western clothes and started to advocate more actively against unjust laws and taxes. Jawaharlal Nehru chose him to become the first Home Minister of India. The museum is set up chronologically and tells the story of his life and his involvement in India's independence struggle. It has some personal artefacts and quite neat models of all the buildings that were at some point associated with him. The four pavilions on the roof of the museum have more galleries on Tagore and the princely states of India, while the basement contains an encyclopaedia-like gallery of important Indians.

6 Circuit House

Opening times: daily, 10am to 5pm
Admission: free

Diagonally across the road from the Sardar Patel National Memorial stands the Circuit House. This two-storey red-brick building is currently in use as a government guesthouse. Cars arrive underneath the central porte-cochere that provides access to the open verandas and loggias. The building is better known, however, not for its architecture but for the events that took place inside it in March 1922. Mahatma Gandhi had propelled the pace of the struggle for independence a few years earlier when he launched a movement that placed emphasis on non-cooperation and non-violence. The strategy worked and the British could think of no adequate response. But then, in February 1922, a section of the Indian National Congress attacked a police station and 22 police officers were killed. Gandhi responded by withdrawing his support from the movement and urged others to do so. Despite this, Gandhi was arrested in March and tried for sedition. On the day of his trial, and to the surprise of all in the court, Gandhi pleaded guilty and told the judge to inflict either the highest penalty possible or to resign his post from the British imperial government. The judge responded with the famous words: "You are in a different category from any person I have ever tried or am likely ever to try . . . in the eyes of millions of your countrymen you are a great patriot and a great leader; even all those who differ from you in politics look up to you as a man of high ideals and of noble and even saintly life." As Gandhi left the judge no choice, he found himself duly sentenced to six years in prison, of which he eventually served two. The room in the Circuit House contains the order, the defence and the judgment of Gandhi in this truly momentous and epoch-making trial.

7 Khan Chishti Masjid

Opening times: dawn to dusk (daily)
Admission: free

The next building lies just across the railway tracks, but unfortunately you will have to walk all the way back to the underpass and then follow the main road in a north-easterly direction for about 200 metres. Head into the lane on the right and follow it all the way to end (around 400 metres). The mosque should look somewhat familiar as it was the basis for the Bibi Achut Kuki Masjid which you saw at the start of this walk. It was built in 1465 on the order of Malik Vazir, who was a nobleman at the court of Mahmud Begada. Like the Bibi Achut Kuki Masjid, the minarets have partly collapsed, but here they have been transformed with new tops, which make them look a little bit like hats. The layout and design of the mosque is typical of the early sultanate style. The central dome is raised above the other two domes and supported by an octagonal arrangement of columns. The columns all have five tiers with three carved elements connecting the two plainer parts. Under the central dome the plainer parts have also been carved.

8 Chinubhai Baronet House

The Chinubhai Baronet House stands quite literally across the compound wall to the south, but again to reach it requires you to head all the way back down the lane and follow the main road back north

for about 400 metres. On the right-hand side is a street on which the towers of Iscon Riverside are located. In a bizarre twist of real-estate management, the front garden of the once grand Chinubhai Baronet House has been sold off for redevelopment into the Iscon development. To reach the house now requires you to ask the guard to let you through to the back (and photography is not allowed). Your patience will be rewarded as the Chinubhai Baronet House is more of a palace than a house. It was designed by the Bengali architect Surendranath in a distinctly Western neoclassical style. It stands on a plinth that is covered in Italian mosaics. The two-storey building has a colonnade with Corinthian capitals all across the front facade. Its corners feature two octagonal tower-like structures that reach three floors and are accessed by two outdoor staircases. The building is in a state of disrepair but many of the original features are still present. The wooden staircases, the window frames and the decorated friezes are all testimony to its former glory.

9 Gandhi Ashram

Opening times: daily, 8.30am to 6.30pm
Admission: free
www.gandhiashramsabarmati.org
+91-79-2755 7277

Head back to the main road and head north towards Subhash Bridge. Cross the river and take a left at the main junction with Ashram Road. Follow the road for about

500 metres due south. It is too hard to overestimate the role Mahatma Gandhi played in India's freedom movement as well as in the country's public imagination. That his image has been on the rupee notes for more than 60 years is a testament to this. When Gandhi returned from South Africa, where he had been working, he first settled in the Kocharab Ashram (see the Kocharab Walk), but in 1917 he shifted to this spot on the Sabarmati river. The ashram was set up around the principles of life, work and religion that Gandhi had formulated and he used it as the headquarters from which he organized the struggle for independence. Gandhi lived in this ashram (also known as Sabarmati Ashram) with his wife and many followers from 1917 to 1930. In 1930, he set out on the Salt March (see also the Ashram Road Walk), during which he vowed not to return to the ashram until India had gained independence. Soon after independence was finally achieved—on August 15, 1947, Gandhi was assassinated, so sadly he never was able to return to his beloved ashram.

The original complex consisted of various buildings that were all important to Gandhi's way of life as well as the principles he taught. Gandhi's notion of *swaraj* or home rule was more than merely freedom from the British; he envisioned a rural lifestyle of flourishing self-sufficient communities that would practice agriculture, animal husbandry and cottage industries to sustain the country and its

people. Gandhi developed a daily schedule that incorporated praying, weaving, reading and other manual labour. He also used the ashram to teach and there is a guest house for those who wished to stay here. Architecturally the buildings are somewhat reminiscent of a simple Indian village. The whitewashed cottages are very much in line with Gandhi's emphasis on simplicity and contain large semi-open *otla*s which form the main gathering spaces within the house. The campus also has the only surviving ghats that lead down to the Sabarmati River.

In 1963 a museum was added to the complex and it houses a large collection of books and articles on Gandhi; it also illustrates his life through text and artefacts. There are 50 hand-drawn panels narrating the key events during Gandhi's time in Ahmedabad. The building was designed by Charles Correa, who conceived of it as a modern interpretation of the Indian village life that Gandhi had advocated. Within a strict orthogonal grid, 51 modular units of 6-by-6 metres have been laid out in an asymmetrical and irregular manner. The periphery of the grid holds the various exhibitions and collections, while the interior grid units are left open to allow light to come in and space for trees as well as a central body of water. The materialization of the building is equally simple: a concrete superstructure, with brick walls and finishes. The ceilings are covered in wooden panels while the floor is made of stone.

🔟 Manav Sadhna Campus

Opening times: daily, dawn to dusk
Admission: free
+91-79-27560002
www.manavsadhna.org

Located inside the sprawling Ramapir No Tekro slum settlement, the Manav Sadhna Campus is not situated on any main road, nor does it have an actual address. Visitors will have to bear this in mind when they make their way through the narrow streets of this vast settlement that is home to more than 150,000 people. Some buildings in Ahmedabad are encroached by slums, but this activity centre was inserted into the settlement to serve the people. The Manav Sadhna organization started operating from Gandhi Ashram, where they would interact and educate slum children on issues of sanitation and personal hygiene. The entire settlement is essentially built upon municipal land around a gully that feeds into the Sabarmati river. The people that live here moved to the city, sometimes decades ago, and are engaged in professions such as pottery, rickshaw driving and day labour. The settlement has plenty of shops, even schools, but lacks many basic municipal services. The Manav Sadhna Campus was built in 2005 and is an effort to remove this imbalance by providing the inhabitants with a training centre and workshop facilities for the production of craft-based products. The buildings are arranged around a large courtyard where trees provide shade for the activities below. The most interesting aspect, however, is that all the materials used in the construction of the building are recycled. Bottles of glass and plastic provide a range of interesting facades. Other walls and doors are made of wooden crates, old CDs or bicycle frames. Even ordinary elements, like the load-bearing structure of bricks and roofs, are built using recycled material. The arrangement and use of materials gives the entire building a playful character. Despite the campus, and years of slow improvement by the people themselves, there are government plans now to demolish the entire settlement. Promises are made to re-house all inhabitants, but the future remains uncertain.

Link to Ashram Road Walk:
Continue walking south along Ashram Road for about 1.5 kilometres (nearly 1 mile) until you reach the intersection with the 120-feet Ring Road.

Ashram Road

Ashram Road takes its name from Mahatma Gandhi's ashram which was located on the city's outskirts. This road runs parallel to the Sabarmati River. At the beginning of the twentieth century this part of the city was still largely agricultural. After the first modern bridge was opened in 1892 it became popular with the British as well as wealthy local industrialists who chose to build their grand new houses on the banks of the river. A number of institutions also chose an address on Ashram Road. Nowadays it has a central place in the city, with the many government buildings on either side and proposals to strengthen its role as a central business district.

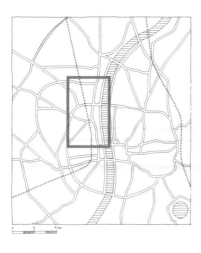

Key

1. Darpana Academy of Performing Arts
2. Sayyid Uthman Masjid
3. Gujarat Vidyapith
4. Sardar Patel Cricket Stadium
5. Reserve Bank of India
6. Heritage bungalows
7. Mill Owners' Association
8. Sabarmati Riverfront
9. Patang Hotel

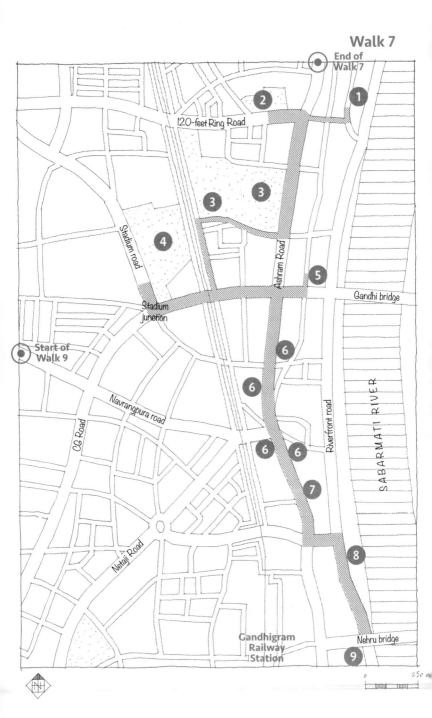

Walk 7

End of
Walk 7

120-feet Ring Road

Stadium road

Ashram Road

Stadium
junction

Gandhi bridge

Start of
Walk 9

Navrangpura road

CG Road

Riverfront road

SABARMATI RIVER

Netaji Road

Gandhigram
Railway
Station

Nehru bridge

0   250 m

111

① Darpana Academy of Performing Arts

Opening times: daily, 10am to 10pm
Admission: free

Natarani Cafe
Opening times: daily, 10am to 10pm
Admission: free
www.darpanaacademy.blogspot.in
+91-79-2755 1389

Close to Usmanpura village lies the campus of the Darpana Academy of Performing Arts. This academy started in 1949 as a school for Indian classical dance. It was conceived by Mrinalini Sarabhai and her scientist husband Vikram Sarabhai. She was a famous Indian classical dancer and choreographer. She started her education as a child in Switzerland and later attended the American Academy of Dramatic Arts. She also trained with Rabindranath Tagore at Santiniketan. In 1968 modernist architect Achyut Kanvinde was commissioned to build the various teaching rooms of the academy. The exposed brick-and-concrete structure is a clear statement of Kanvinde's functionalist ideology. This building opens onto the rear of the Natarani Theatre; a playful open-air theatre built in 1994 and incorporating an existing tree. It is currently being revamped to accommodate more people. The front of the building has two other, newer additions. The first is an office that re-uses the old wooden facade of a *haveli*. Wrapped around the other side of the building are the curved brick seating arrangements of the Natarani Cafe. Apart from Indian classical dance, the complex also now teaches a number of other performing arts and plays host to several international festivals. Since 1977 it has been headed by the founders' daughter Mallika Sarabhai.

② Sayyid Uthman Masjid

Opening times: daily, dawn to dusk
Admission: free

This mosque, also close to Usmanpura village, is the only historic Muslim place of worship on the western bank of the Sabarmati River. The mosque not only has a unique location but it also marks a stylistic break with mosques built earlier in Ahmedabad. The minarets, which are usually placed next to a mosque's main entrance, are here placed at either end of the front facade, and this is no longer a wall punctuated by openings but is completely open, supported only by columns, and there are no arches anywhere in the mosque. These architectural changes coincide with the beginning of the reign of Mahmud Begada in 1458, two years before the construction on this mosque began. It takes its name from Sayyid Uthman, a Sufi who was performing miracles in the village he founded and which still bears his name. The man clearly had a strong influence, and Mahmud Begada was a religious man, so both mosque and the Sufi's tomb were financed and constructed by Mahmud Begada. One of the two most important

sultans of Ahmedabad (along with Ahmedabad's founder Ahmed Shah), Begada's long reign lasted for 43 years and was influential. He expanded the Gujarat Sultanate to include the Malwa region, west of Gujarat. He is best known for the city that was rebuilt in this region, Champaner, which had a history dating back to the eighth century.

After Begada captured the Pavagadh Fort above the city, he renamed it Muhammadabad and spent 23 years rebuilding it. The architectural style of the buildings in Champaner is similar to the buildings in Ahmedabad as they were constructed at the same time. Champaner's buildings, however, reflect the older style of the Sultanate unlike the newer style found here in the Sayyid Uthman Masjid. Champaner is now a UNESCO World Heritage site. It lies 160 kilometres south-east of Ahmedabad and can be reached from the nearest city of Vadodara on a day trip. Mahmud Begada was also the Sultan when the Portuguese arrived in 1498, under the command of Vasco da Gama. They had captured various places along the Indian Ocean coast but the Gujaratis were still in control of the Gulf of Cambay. To secure uninterrupted trade between the Spice Islands (today's Ternate, Tidore, Moti, etc.) and the European mainland, the Portuguese felt it essential to control this part of the Indian Ocean and in 1509 the two powers met at Diu for a naval battle. The Gujarat Sultanate was supported by the Ottoman Empire and even the Republic of Venice, who were both keen on limiting the Portuguese power. Despite this coalition of forces the Gujarat Sultanate lost the battle at Diu and Gujarat was cut off from the sea.

3 Gujarat Vidyapith

Opening times: Daily, 10am to 6pm
Admission: free

Navajivan Trust
Opening times: Monday to Saturday, 10.30am to 5.30pm
Admission: free

Retrace your steps to Ashram Road and take a right. Follow the road for 400 metres until you reach the entrance gate of the Gujarat Vidyapith on your right. This university was founded by Mahatma Gandhi in 1920 on basis of the idea that India should have an independent educational institute outside of British influence. The university would train students in accordance with Gandhi's principles and provide graduates capable of ruling an independent India. The number of students quickly swelled to 30,000 in the first few years of its existence. Then, during the period of civil obedience and the Quit India Movement, the university was closed and students were encouraged to join in. The campus is spread over eight hectares (20 acre) of land and includes colleges, a library, hostels and sports grounds. The main architectural interest is primarily the boys' hostel, located to the rear of the campus. This two-storey hostel is set around a large courtyard with several mature trees. There is an open walkway with Corinthian capitals connecting all the rooms. There are gated entrances and staircases at the four cardinal points. Upon leaving the campus, take a right, then another right so that you are walking alongside the boundary of the Gujarat Vidyapith. Continue to walk for 300 metres until you reach the **Navajivan Trust building**. The building itself is not terribly distinctive but inside it is preserved the original printing press that Gandhi, and various colleagues, used to print the weekly Hindi-language *Navajivan*, a journal started in 1919 to propagate the idea of self-rule. The building also has a shop selling books on Gandhi, and a cafe.

4 Sardar Patel Cricket Stadium

Opening times: daily, 10am to 5pm
Admission: free

Keep walking until you see the railroad underpass. Behind the tracks stands the Sardar Patel Cricket Stadium (the main entrance is on the other side of the stadium, along Stadium Road). In the early 1950s, just a few years after Indian independence, the municipality commissioned Charles Correa to design a new cricket stadium. A huge parcel of land was gifted by the province of Bombay (the state of Gujarat was formed only in 1960) for the realization of a stadium with capacity for 35,000 people. Construction of the stadium started in 1959. It was decided to abandon plans for the roof to cover the seating due to lack of funds, and the stadium was finished in 1966. The stadium had the honour of

hosting the first One Day International cricket match between India and England in 1981 (which also, incidentally, turned out to be the last One Day International ever to be played here). The seating is arranged on a sculptural harmonica-shaped concrete structure that stretches 700 metres around the entire 230-metre diameter of the stadium. Its innovative structural design of reinforced concrete was conceived by Mahendra Raj, India's most well-known structural engineer. A stretch of 120 metres on the south side is completely finished, including its reinforced-concrete cantilever roof. In 1987, another Sardar Patel Stadium opened (which is commonly known as the Motera stadium) to meet with new standards and offered an increased capacity. The first stadium still hosts Gujarat cricket team's matches in the Ranji Trophy (a national-level cricket championship played between teams representing regional cricket associations).

5 Reserve Bank of India

Head south towards CG road and follow it till you reach the intersection with Ashram Road. This busy junction (commonly known as Income-Tax crossroads) has a **statue of Mahatma Gandhi** that commemorates the start of the Salt March on 12th March 1930. In this 241-mile march, Gandhi protested against the British salt laws by walking to the coast and making salt. Thousands of Indians followed his example and the British jailed more than 60,000 people in the subsequent weeks. The march also marked Gandhi's departure from Ahmedabad as he swore not to return to the Ashram till Independence was achieved. The bridge across the Sabarmati river built near here in 1952 is named after Gandhi. Slightly ahead of the junction, towards Gandhi Bridge, stands the **Reserve Bank of India**. It was built in 1975 by the architect Hasmukh Patel. Apart from offices, the building has storage space for currency and is therefore highly protected. The main seven-storey tower stands on a high three-storey podium and is oriented north-south to reduce the impact of the sun. The window bays are recessed to further reduce it. The open space on top of the podium contains gardens for the employees and is connected to the entrance plaza by a ceremonial staircase.

⑥ Heritage bungalows

Head back to Ashram Road and take a left. This road is home to a large number of heritage bungalows. When the new Ellis Bridge opened in 1892 many wealthy families decided to move from their townhouses in the old city to bungalows in this newer part of the city. Unlike other new areas to the east of the old city, which were associated with textile mills and workers' housing, this area across the river provided the well-to-do with a clean and quiet environment. The stretch of road between the Mill Owners' Association and CG Road has a cluster of four particularly interesting homes. The whitewashed **Rang Jyot Bungalow** appears on the left side of the road around 200-metres south of the CG Road junction. This two-storey bungalow has three wings, each 120-degrees apart, and is designed in the fashionable modern movement style of the 1930s and 1940s. Next, diagonally across from the Rang Jyot Bungalow stands **Sorab Villa**. Built in 1939, this is also executed in the modern style, with rounded rooms on its corners. Next to Sorab Villa stands **NTC House**, which is more classical in design. Its large porch provides a ceremonial entrance for the cars and carriages arriving to visit the National Textile Cooperation, which is housed here now. Continue walking south towards a busy T-junction where you will see a small Hindu shrine. Just after the junction, on the right-hand side, stands the **School for Deaf Mutes**. Erected here in 1928 with the specific aim of educating deaf-mute children, the modest buildings, with pitched roofs, are arranged around a central courtyard. It is still in operation to this day. Finally, diagonally across from this school stands another heritage bungalow dating from 1908. Its owner opened a small restaurant in the garden, so you will be able to sit and enjoy the wooden architecture of three-storey bungalow with large veranda and pitched roof.

7 Mill Owners' Association

Opening times: Monday to Friday, 10.30am to 3.45pm,
Saturday, 10.30am to 11.45am
Admission: free
www.atmaahd.wordpress.com
+91-79-26582273

On the adjacent plot, on the left-hand side of the road you will see the imposing concrete facade of the Mill Owners' Association. This office and convention building is one of the four works realized by Le Corbusier in Ahmedabad. While working on the capitol complex in Chandigarh, Le Corbusier was introduced to several of Jawaharlal Nehru's influential friends in Ahmedabad (he made a total of 23 trips to India). Surottam Hutheesing, who was the president of the Mill Owners' Association, commissioned him to design their new headquarters. The two residential projects that Le Corbusier also designed, the Shodhan House and the Sarabhai House, are private residences and not open to the public. The Mill Owners' Association building was finished in 1954 which makes it Le Corbusier's first completed work in the city. It exemplifies all the key architectural ideas that Corbusier developed through his earlier work and manages to adapt them to local climate and customs. As such, it represents a synthesis between modern architecture and a local embedding that has been an inspiration for generations of architects ever since. You enter the building via a gently sloping ramp that takes you to the first floor, where the view is broken by a blind wall. The experience of the ascent is tightly controlled. The brises-soleils have been placed at such an angle that it is not possible to look inside the building when approaching it. These sun screens are an effective tool to help shade the building and yet allow cooling breeze to blow through, both especially important considerations in the hot dry climate of Ahmedabad. The spaces between the sun screens are filled with planting. The rear facade uses the same brises-soleils but the angle here is perpendicular to the facade, which allows for a full view of the river behind. The river used to run to the edge of the site during the rainy season but now a road cuts across it. The roof is an integral part of the building and can be accessed via a small stairs on the side. Two skylights provide lighting for rooms below. It is very common in Ahmedabad for people to use their roofs at the end of the day, when the sun is going down, to catch the cooling evening breezes. This building was built primarily from exposed concrete but on the inside the walls are covered with plaster and selectively painted in a red paint. The lower outside walls are exposed brick. Inside the building, a small exhibition shows some of the information about it, including plans and several inspiring

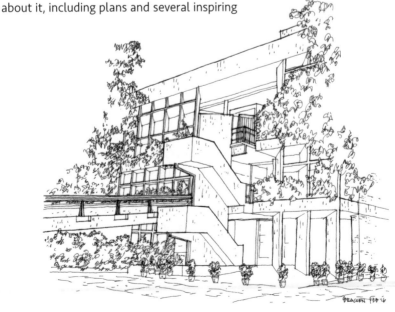

quotes from Le Corbusier. There is also a map of the 64 cotton mills that once functioned in Ahmedabad and which directly provided the money for the construction of this masterpiece.

8 Sabarmati Riverfront

After leaving the Mill Owners' Association take a left and you will see the **Shiv Cinema** which was established here in 1973 and is one of the oldest cinemas still in operation in the city. After passing the cinema, take a left and walk up to the Sabarmati river. The riverfront is a colossal redevelopment project covering more than 20 kilometre of riverbank. The Sabarmati is now a seasonal river and its riverbed is dry for most of the year. During the monsoon, however, the river swells and intermittently floods the riverbanks. The first proposal to tackle this problem came from French architect Bernard Kohn in 1961 but was never realized. The idea re-emerged in 1997 when funds became available from Central government. The main objective of the project was three-fold: first, change the Sabarmati River from a seasonal stream into a permanent waterbody by building a dam at the southern edge of the city; second, transform the waterfront from private ownership into a public space by reclaiming 160 hectares (400 acres) of land from the river; and finally, solve the problem of periodic flooding of the river once and for all. The design of the riverbank is a simple concrete retaining wall that uniformly aligns with the water. The land above this retaining wall is used for public spaces, and as a land bank to help finance the project. The project also encompasses new roads along the waterfront. The water inside the new city-lake is being fed by a large agricultural canal that connects it to the Narmada river in southern Gujarat. The project has received international praise for its scope and scale, especially because it was the first time that something like this had been built in India. However, there was also some criticism because of the process by which more than 50,000 people were relocated, and the environmental effects of the dam downstream.

⑨ Patang Hotel

Opening times: daily, 11.30am to 2.30pm and 7 to 10.30pm
Admission: free
www.neelkanthpatang.com
+91-79-6661 4154

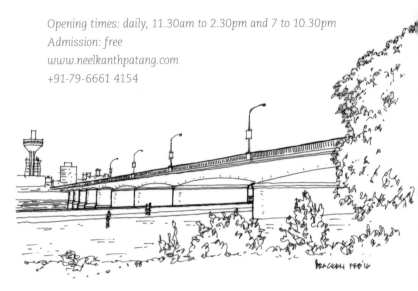

Continue the walk by heading south along the waterfront. Even before reaching Nehru Bridge the lollipop-shaped Patang Tower will be clearly visible all the way along the river. Built in 1980, this tower is one of the most recognizable landmarks of Ahmedabad. The tower, which is a hotel, and the adjacent office building are both part of the Chinubhai Centre designed by Hasmukh Patel. The Centre's main idea was to maximize views of the river in both the tower and the adjacent office block. The 67-metre high tower was designed with a rotating restaurant. The floor of this conical-shaped restaurant makes a full circle in 90 minutes. The trapezoidal office block has a standardized plan of a central corridor connecting the elevators to the offices. The unique feature of the building is that each floor is stepped back to create shady terraces with views across the water.

Link to University Walk:
Follow Ashram Road back to Navrangpura Road, then head left towards Commerce six-roads junction.

Ahmedabad is home to some of the best educational institutes in the country. Most of these institutes are clustered in the university area. The history of the area can be traced back at least to 1935, when the Ahmedabad Education Society started constructing the first colleges. Although the idea to establish a proper university was already floated before Independence, it only became possible after the British finally left in 1947. A huge amount of land had been bought, and industrialists like Kasturbhai, and later, Vikram Sarabhai started to attract new institutions and new architects to the city. In the early 1960s the university extended rapidly with the establishment of the L.D. Institute of Indology (1961), Centre for Environmental Planning and Technology (1962) and the Indian Institute of Management, Ahmedabad (1962). These buildings provided great opportunities for modern architects to show how their ideas about architecture would be reflected in educational institutes. The present university and its affiliated institutes constitute a sprawling organization that has more than 200,000 students.

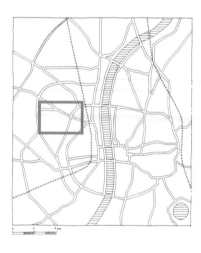

Key

1. Institute of Engineering and Technology
2. Centre for Environmental Planning and Technology
3. Amdavad ni Gufa
4. Gujarat University
5. L.D. Institute of Indology
6. Newman Hall
7. Hollywood slum
8. Birds and Beasts Asylum
9. Ahmedabad Management Association
10. Indian Institute of Management, Ahmedabad

Walk 9

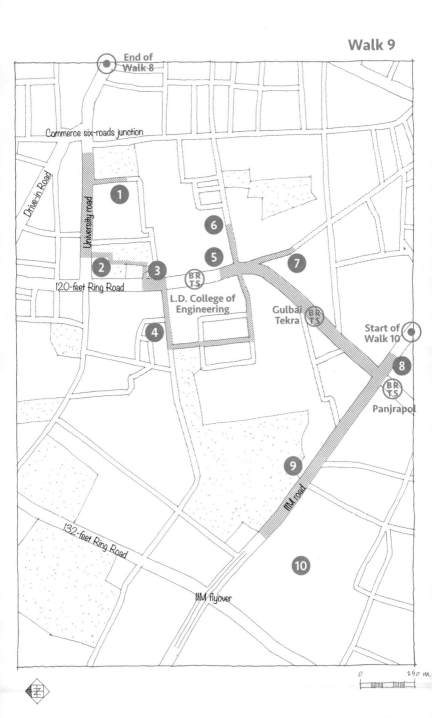

End of Walk 8

Commerce six-roads junction

Drive-in Road

University road

1

6

5

2

3

BR TS

7

120-feet Ring Road

L.D. College of Engineering

4

Gulbai Tekra

BR TS

Start of Walk 10

8

BR TS

Panjrapol

9

IIM road

132-feet Ring Road

10

IIM flyover

0   250 m

① Institute of Engineering and Technology

The easiest way to find the start of this walk is to head to Commerce six-roads intersection. From here, walk up University Road for some 200 metres and take a left to enter the compound of the Institute of Engineering and Technology. Completed at the end of 2015, the Institute of Engineering and Technology is the latest addition to the vast complex of Gujarat University and its affiliated institutes. This building looks rather bulky from the outside but is actually set up around a courtyard in a manner similar to earlier college buildings. Four orthogonal axes offer views to the outside and divide the building into nine unequal parts offering a range of different-sized classrooms around the central courtyard. The building, which was designed by Delhi-based vir.mueller architects, also emulates the exposed concrete structure of many earlier Modernist buildings in Ahmedabad. Instead of brick, though, the entire building is clad in red sandstone screens to keep out the summer heat. Larger classrooms on the eastern facade are shaded by an enormous concrete slab that is supported by a four-storey high W-shaped frame. Within the same grounds as the institute stands the **L.D. Arts College**. This college was set up in 1937 as one of the first in Gujarat University, a mere two years after the Ahmedabad Education Society was set up. The college was named after Lalbhai Dalpatbhai, the father of the industrialist Kasturbhai Lalbhai who was involved in the founding of the college.

② Centre for Environmental Planning and Technology

Opening times: daily, 9am to 9pm
Admission: free
www.cept.ac.in

Hutheesing Visual Arts Centre
Opening times: daily, 11am to 8pm
Admission: free
www.umanghutheesing.com

The Kanoria Art Centre
Opening times: daily, 11am to 3.30pm (closed Sunday)
Admission: free
www.kanoriacentreforarts.org
+91-79-26308727

Chauraha cafe
Opening times: daily, 10am to 7pm (closed on Sunday)
Admission: free

Head back to the main road and take a left. After 300 metres you will find the entrance to the Centre for Environmental Planning and Technology (CEPT), an ever-expanding campus established by architect B.V. Doshi for the Ahmedabad Education Society. The campus started with the School of Architecture, conceived in 1962 and built four years later. After this, the School of Planning (1972), School of Building Science and Technology (1982), and School for Interior Design (1992) were all established as well as the more recent School of Management. Even now the campus is still expanding, with plans for a new library.

The **School of Architecture** consists of a series of studios raised above the ground to create a shaded multifunctional space. The form of the building was meant to encourage the free flow of ideas and interaction between the students and the faculty members. Doshi intended for the school to be not just a place where students would follow classes but one that would allow other ways of teaching and learning as well. The studios were constructed as large open spaces without doors, and the large full-storey-height windows that are usually open. The studios are constructed as a series of parallel bays facing north-south to minimize the impact of the sun. Large north-facing skylights bring light into the studios, while the double-height spaces allow further cooling. Large brises-soleils along the facade, similar to the ones used in the Mill Owners' Building, allow the breeze to come in, but keep the sun out. The building is constructed out of plain load-bearing exposed brickwork and exposed concrete. In front of the school, facing the northern facade of the school, are a series of curve-edged lawns, which are

best enjoyed in the late afternoon and evening. A series of steps link the School of Architecture with the **School of Planning** and the administrative department. Together, they form an L-shaped building that loosely defines a large open space at the centre of the campus.

Diagonally opposite to the central open space stands the **Hutheesing Visual Arts Centre**. The idea of the institution for the promotion of arts and culture was based on the structure of Santiniketan, the university that Rabindranath Tagore established in West Bengal. The centre organizes exhibitions, workshops and performances in many different art forms. Its architectural language is similar to that of CEPT, again with the use of exposed brick and concrete.

To the rear of the Visual Arts Centre stand the **School of Building Science and Technology** and **School of Interior Design**. These buildings define yet another open space, informally linked with the others. A series of platforms of brick form a small-size amphitheatre, where students sometime put up performances. CEPT is always buzzing, so check the notice boards if there might be a lecture or event you can attend.

Continue past the stationery shop at the western side of the central open ground and you will find the **Kanoria Art Centre**. This is an exhibition space, with attached library and cafe, and was also designed by Doshi and opened in 2011. The exhibition space is long and primarily intended to display paintings and drawings. Light comes from above, through the narrow slit between the walls and the concrete-slab roof. The building's exterior is of exposed brick, matching the buildings of the School of Architecture. It has frequent exhibitions, mostly free of charge; the schedule is available online.

③ Amdavad ni Gufa

Opening times: daily, 10am to 8pm
Admission: free

Zen cafe
Opening times: daily, 4pm to 8pm

The Amdavad ni Gufa can be reached easily from the CEPT campus by heading south from the Hutheesing Visual Arts Centre for about 100 metres. The Gufa is probably the most unconventional piece of

architecture in the city, as its form bears no resemblance to anything created here before. Its tortoise-like shell gives it an other-worldly appearance, and its interior is as unique as its exterior. Ocular skylights dimly illuminate the brightly coloured paintings that cover the curved walls.

The building is a collaboration between long-time friends architect B.V. Doshi and artist Maqbool Fida Husain. In the early 1990s, Husain asked Doshi to find a location and to design a gallery suitable for his artwork. Doshi was inspired by the use of subterranean spaces in his earlier works and this time aimed at employing the spiritual quality of subterranean space to achieve a feeling reminiscent of the ancient rock caves of western India. Although contemporary in form, the Gufa—or cave—shows Doshi's ability to support the modern with the ancient. The domes and their supports were constructed from ferro-cement and have been covered with mosaics of china to deflect the harsh sunlight. A black snake-like motif runs all the way around the dome's exterior. The artwork inside evokes early human wall painting or perhaps an Indian version of Plato's cave. Outside the art gallery is a lovely cafe called the Zen cafe that serves excellent coffee, for a moment of architectural contemplation before walking back out onto the busy main road.

4 Gujarat University

Exit the Gufa onto the 120-feet Ring Road and you will be able to see the tower at the heart of Gujarat University. This hexagonal clock tower is the symbolic centre of the campus. The history of the university can be traced back to the 1920s, when Indians were promoting the idea of their own universities. An important step in that process was the establishment of the Ahmedabad Education Society in 1935. This organization was formed by some of Ahmedabad's most influential citizens, like the industrialist Kasturbhai Lalbhai. They realized that India and its industries could only flourish if new people were trained not in faraway London but right here in Ahmedabad.

Already in 1936 a commerce college had been opened, and soon after that, an arts college. After the British finally left India in 1947 there were no more barriers for a university to open, and this was one of the first two in Gujarat, established in November 1949 (the Maharaja Sayajirao University of Baroda was also established in 1949, April).

The main building has three wings protruding outwards from the central clock tower. The main entrance sits in a three-storey block located between two of these wings and faces east. The entire building is clad in sandstone with some red sandstone highlights. Leave the clock tower building to the south and take right. After 100 metres you will come to the entrance of **L.D. College of Engineering**. This college is one of the oldest on the campus. The classrooms are arranged a bit like barracks but the feel of the campus is actually quite pleasant, with trees shading the informal spaces between the red-brick buildings.

⑤ L.D. Institute of Indology

Lalbhai Dalpatbhai Museum
Opening times: daily, 10.30am to 5.30pm (except Mondays)
Admission: free
www.ldmuseum.in
+91-79-26306883

You can exit the campus of L.D. College of Engineering from the southern side, emerging back onto 120-feet Ring Road. Straight across the road is the entrance of the L.D. Institute of Indology. Set in a lush garden set back from the main road, the Institute of Indology is a celebration of Indian culture, both in the collection of the museum as well as in the architecture of the building. The museum houses a collection of Indian sculpture, paintings, manuscripts and coins that have been donated by various benefactors over the years. The first of such gifts was by a Jain monk named Muni Shri Punyavijayji in the 1950s. He approached wealthy industrialist Kasturbhai Lalbhai and together they formed a proposal to build a research institute and museum on a piece of land that was donated by the Ahmedabad Education Society.

The building is divided in a lower (partly subterranean) part that houses the art collection and an upper one that contains the library, teaching facilities and administration. Because the precious manuscripts and paintings would degrade under the influence of direct sunlight and the moist air of central air-conditioning, their storage has been placed underground. To let light in for the display of the documents, sculptural protruding skylights have been placed on either side of the space to allow indirect lighting. The light in fact reflects off the pool—which is filled every monsoon—in front of the building. The remainder of the building's accommodation was placed on top of the naturally cooled museum. The second floor is cantilevered over the first to provide shading. There are many other fine details in this building's architecture, including the balustrades that double up as benches, or the protruding water spouts on the corners that let out the monsoon rainfall, just like the ceremonial fluids that were dispensed using idols in ancient Indian temples.

In 1984 a new extension was added to the building and in 1993 a second new wing was added to the rear to house a collection of Indian miniature paintings previously displayed at Le Corbusier's Sanskar

Kendra. As in all the buildings by B.V. Doshi, the architecture is a cross-fertilization of ancient Indian and modern architectural expression. The concrete construction and detailing is distinctly modern, while the organization of the spaces and the climatological concepts refer back to much older local architectural traditions. The Institute of Indology was the first institutional building that he conceived of as an independent architect and, as such, formed a precedent for his buildings to come, where he re-used many of its forms and ideas. The museum's collection features objects going back to the fifth century. Many major Indian dynasties (Gupta, Chola and Mughal) and religions (Jain, Buddhist and Hindu) are represented which allows for the opportunity to explore changes in styles, materials and iconography.

6 Newman Hall

Upon exiting the L.D. Institute of Indology, continue walking along 120-feet Ring Road around the block heading east. After 300 metres you will find Newman Hall. This hostel is for the priests from the St. Xavier's College, which stands across the road. The hostel is a simple three-storey structure of exposed brick and concrete organized in an H-shaped plan. The priests' rooms open onto an arcade of narrow brick walls that also act as shading devices. The plan forms two courtyards, both of which are shaded by leafy trees. Inside the western courtyard is a small chapel, also constructed from brick. The building was designed by Ahmedabad-based architect Hasmukh C. Patel.

7 Hollywood slum

Retrace your steps back towards the 120-feet Ring Road and keep to the left, as the road bends away from the Ring Road. After 200 metres you will come to an informal settlement known colloquially as the Hollywood *basti* (slum), and part of Gulbai Tekra area. Inhabitants mainly come from Rajasthan and claim to have started living here more than one hundred years ago. Whether or not this is true is not really all that important; the main activity the settlement is known for and also its main source of livelihood is the making of Lord Ganesha idols for the Ganesh Chaturthi festival. Ganesha is readily recognizable by his elephant head (and big belly) and is known as the remover of obstacles and a patron of the arts and sciences. The idols are made from clay, painted and decorated. 'Hollywood' is a popular destination for the Ahmedabadi devotees to buy an idol of the god on the occasion of Ganesh Chaturthi. The festival ends on the tenth day when the idol is taken in a festive procession to a lake, river or sea and immersed in it. The festival usually comes in either August or September (depending on the phase of the moon), so the best time to see these Ganeshas in production is in the months beforehand.

8 Birds and Beasts Asylum

Make your way back to the 120-feet Ring Road and follow in a southerly direction for about 600 metres till you reach the Panjrapol junction. The junction takes its name from the Birds and Beasts Asylum (or Panjrapol in Gujarati), whose entrance is across the road on the left-hand side where there is a simple gate featuring two cows drinking from a fountain. Head inside and you will stumble across a large slab stating that the foundation stone for the asylum was laid in 1929 by Chinubhai Ranchhodlal. From the slab it is also possible to establish that the building was opened in 1932 by another industrialist, Kasturbhai.

The building was established by the Maskati cloth market, an influential trading house (the centre of operations is close to the railway station and can be visited in the Station Area Walk). The central feature of the asylum is a five-storey grey-and-pink administration building-cum-clock tower. The building feels a bit boxy, with heavy-looking pilasters on its corners. Apart from the clock's hands, the building is fortunately still intact, with all its balustrades and window shutters still in place. The asylum has long since been closed and much of its grounds are covered in weeds but you can see where the animals used to be held in a series of bays which fan outwards. At present some people have taken up residence in the animal enclosures, although it seems like their cows are the ones who feel more at home than their owners.

9 Ahmedabad Management Association

From the Birds and Beasts Asylum turn left, cross the 120-feet Ring Road and head along IIM Road for 400 metres. The Ahmedabad Management Association will be on your right and is an organization that provides management training and also space for large-scale events. It was built in 1999 by architect Bimal Patel, who is also responsible for the new campus of Indian Institute of Management, Ahmedabad. The building here basically operates as one long corridor accessed via two-storey entrances, both of which feature carved metal decoration. A ramp leads to the second floor which gives access to a library and large auditorium. The facade has circular windows and was originally executed in exposed concrete; this has now unfortunately been covered up by some rather dull-looking grey paint.

10 Indian Institute of Management, Ahmedabad

Farther along IIM Road on the left is the Indian Institute of Management, Ahmedabad. After the Independence of India in 1947 there was a growing need to train people to lead the country and set up and manage new companies. Leading industrialists like Vikram Sarabhai and Kasturbhai Lalbhai took a leading role in the conceptualization of a new Indian Institute of Management (IIM) that was modelled on the Harvard Business School. One of the key features was a Western-style education system that would allow for discussion and debate with the aim of forming more critically aware students. The IIM Ahmedabad, whose logo is based on the *jaali* of the Sidi Saiyed Masjid in the Bhadra area of the old city, is now part of 19 such schools across India. It is the second oldest, established only a few months after the first IIM in Calcutta in 1961.

The architectural work was initially offered to B.V. Doshi but he recommended that Louis Kahn design the building. Kahn was already working on another building on the Indian subcontinent, the National Assembly of Bangladesh, which meant that he was already familiar with local climate, building materials and construction methods.

The 24-hectare campus is divided into a large monumental academic building that contains the library and all teaching rooms, and a residential area that houses both students and staff and radiates from the main building. The academic building is organized around a large plaza—known as Louis Kahn Plaza—which has a sober monumentality. Its western wing contains six classrooms while the eastern has faculty staff offices. These two wings are connected via the four-storey library. The classrooms are organized around a number of courtyards, which let in the light and allow air to circulate.

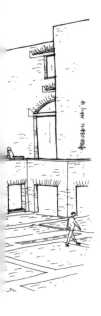

The building uses simple primary shapes and has a simple exposed-brick and concrete structure. One of its most distinctive features is the use of brick arches held together by concrete beams. The housing is conceived in a similar architectural language to the academic block, but on a smaller scale. Each student dormitory is identically arranged in such a way as to form a chequered pattern of courtyards. Rooms are organized around an open triangular-shaped lobby which gives access to bathrooms on opposite corners. The entire complex has an austere quality reminiscent of some of the lost cities of India, like Mandu, Madhya Pradesh, now only ruins. It is not too fanciful to think that Kahn might have intended the visitor to feel like they were walking through an ancient fortress, as it is known that he had earlier been inspired by castles in Europe, seen on his travels. The style and organization of the space has been very influential for Indian architects, for example, the distinctive way a small slid is left open at either side of the balustrades is widely copied and has become an almost colloquial part of Ahmedabadi architecture.

Access to the campus is restricted and by prior appointment only. But the IIM Ahmedabad also organizes several annual festivals which are open to all. The entire campus has been slowly expanding over the decades since it was built, with new housing being added around the original hostel buildings and an additional campus built across the main road that opened in 2009. The design by Bimal Patel has tried to emulate the original housing blocks to meet the campus's new requirements.

Link to the Kocharab Walk:
Follow the IIM road back towards Parimal Garden, then head left towards Law Garden.

Kocharab lies on the western bank of the Sabarmati river. Kocharab and its neighbouring area, Paldi, were small settlements at the time when Ahmedabad was still contained within its city walls. Kocharab literally means 'settlement of the Arabs'. Before the introduction of paper Indians used palm leaves to write. When paper was first introduced, its production was dominated by people from the Muslim community. Kocharab village emerged as a paper-manufacturing hub but in the latter part of the nineteenth century, competition from British machine-made paper forced them all out of business. With direct access to the old city, this area also saw a range of new institutions built here at this time and right into the beginning of the twentieth century. Today it remains a hub for all kinds of cultural institutions.

Key

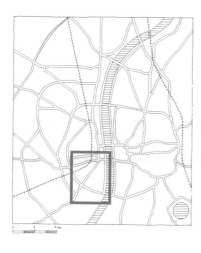

1. Law Garden
2. Gujarat United School of Theology
3. Gujarat Arts and Science College
4. Art Book Center
5. Mangaldas Girdhardas Town Hall
6. Maneklal Jethabhai Library
7. Vadilal Sarabhai Hospital
8. Kocharab Ashram
9. National Institute of Design
10. Sanskar Kendra
11. Tagore Memorial Hall

Walk 10

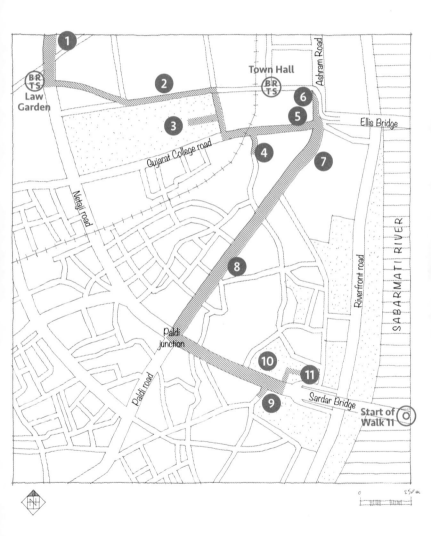

1 Law Garden

Law Garden market
Opening times: dusk to 11pm
Admission: free

At the centre of this busy commercial area lies Law Garden. Named after a nearby law college, the streets adjoining the garden have transformed themselves in recent years into one of the main market areas of the city. The easiest way to reach Law Garden market is via the Law Garden BRTS stand. This evening market offers a wide range of traditional clothing and handicraft items and even has an informal food court.

To continue the walk, leave Law Garden market via Netaji Road in southerly direction. On the corner stands the **Bhaikaka Bhawan,** a conference center re-designed by architect Hasmukh Patel. The two parts of the centre appear as extruded masses, forming an informal break-out space in between them. Take a left and follow the BRTS route in an easterly direction. Along this road, lined with lush trees, stand several interesting **heritage bungalows** dating from the beginning of the twentieth century. All of them have incorporated stylistic elements from the Western neoclassical tradition in their architecture.

2 Gujarat United School of Theology

Opening times: daily, 6am to 6pm
Admission: free
+91-94-29438334

Continue walking along the BRTS corridor for 600 metres until you see the Gujarat United School of Theology on your left. This school was built in 1913 by the Irish Presbyterian Church and still functions as a place where pastors are trained.

The buildings of the school essentially form a courtyard, with two wings on either side containing student rooms and a main building in front with chapel and classrooms. The four houses for the teachers are arranged at either ends of the student housing, connected via a spacious veranda. The whole complex is designed in a neo-gothic style, with red brick, arched windows and merlons on their parapets. The main building contains some interesting stone *jaali* carving showing various Christian motifs. The central carving contains the Indian lotus and the Irish three-leafed shamrock (a type of clover). The interior of the building (ask someone to open it if the door is closed) still contains all its original wooden furniture (a lot of it featuring the shamrock) and some nice mosaics, which are thought to be Italian. In 1973 a library was added to the rear by architect Christopher Benninger for the Alliance Française, a training centre for French language education and culture. The exposed brick building is made up of two interlocking squares positioned to face the side of the church. Light is allowed in via north-facing skylights. The rear facade lavatories pop out of the building like turrets. Alliance Française moved to a new premise in 2013.

③ Gujarat Arts and Science College

Opening times: daily, 9am to 5pm
Admission: free (photography not allowed)

After leaving the Gujarat United School of Theology cross the road and take a left where you will find yourself walking alongside a flyover until you reach the next junction, at which you should take a right. After 70 metres the entrance to the campus of the Gujarat Arts and Science College will be on your right.

This college is one of the oldest educational institutes in the state of Gujarat, founded in 1860 by a British national called Mr. Hope. It predates the foundation of Gujarat University, to which it is currently affiliated. The present buildings on the campus all date from after 1872, when the college was restarted by Sheth Ranchhodlal after five years of inactivity. The Ranchhodlal family donated funds for construction as well as more than 15 hectares (37 acres) of land. The first building constructed was the Arts College, which still forms the main building on campus. To find it from the entrance, follow the central access lane west. There is a botanical garden on your left, which, unfortunately, is in a state of disrepair. The red-brick facade of the Arts College is divided into two wings either side of a central porch. The building is an eclectic combination of different juxtaposed elements. Two rows of arcades are terminated at either end by round castle-like towers containing the stairs. The roof and the central clock tower have a timber framework structure.

Another building of interest is Gandhi Hall, to the left of the main college. This was erected in 1920 in a form reminiscent of a chapel. Behind the main building are situated a newer arts college, library, hostels and sports area. The college has some notable alumni, including the industrialist Kasturbhai Lalbhai, the scientist Vikram Sarabhai and the poet Kavi Dalpatram. A historic moment was recorded here in 1920 when Mahatma Gandhi held a mass meeting to try and convince the students to join his non-cooperation movement.

When the college fell under the control of the British government many students left to join the independent university founded by Gandhi, the Gujarat Vidyapith.

4 Art Book Center

Admission: free
www.artbookcenter.net/about.htm
+91-79-2658 2130

Leave the campus of the Gujarat Arts and Science College and take a right. Then take a left at the next junction and pass underneath the railway bridge. Take the first lane to the right; this winds upwards towards the brightly coloured facade of the Art Book Center. The upper part of this 100-year-old house has a fantastic collection of books on architecture, design and art. In 1970 the owner of the building, who had been working for various bookstores, opened up part of his house as a part-time bookstore. Since then, the collection has been growing slowly but steadily. The shop is particularly specialized in books on Indian textiles and Indian miniatures paintings, but also has books on Ahmedabadi architecture as well as architects who have worked in Ahmedabad, like Le Corbusier and Louis Kahn.

The owner will surely be able to guide you to a book on any topic related to the arts and since he has retired from his regular job, the shop is now open every day of the week from 10am to 6pm The entrance is to the left-hand side of the house.

5 Mangaldas Girdhardas Town Hall

Head back to the main road and take a right. After 200 metres you will come to a large junction with a flyover. Facing this junction stands the Mangaldas Girdhardas Town Hall. After the completion of Ellis Bridge in 1892 many new buildings came to be built in this area in subsequent decades. This red-brick town hall, appropriately, faces the bridge head on. The building was designed by Mumbai-based architect Claude Bartley in 1938. He headed the Architecture Department at the J.J. School of Art in Mumbai, in which the curriculum focused on a classic architectural education that emphasized a symmetrical, orderly layout, harmonious proportions and sculptural decorative elements. The town hall exemplifies the Indo-Saracenic style of architecture that fuses elements of British colonial and native Indian architecture. The cross-shaped first two floors of red brick form the base for an octagonal structure supporting the central dome. This is crowned with a lantern letting in light to the assembly space below. The eaves extending across the parapet of the building offer protection from the sun for the windows below and incorporate Indian-style grills. The town hall was named after the prominent textile mill owner Mangaldas, whose former residence is across the bridge in Bhadra.

6 Maneklal Jethabhai Library

Opening times: daily, 10am to 6pm
Admission: free

Directly adjacent to the Mangaldas Girdhardas Town Hall stands the whitewashed Maneklal Jethabhai Library. The architectural style of this building shows the wide range of interpretations possible for the Indo-Saracenic style, which blends elements from both Indian and

Western architecture. The library was constructed in 1938 with funds donated by Rasiklal Maneklal. The book collection was initially begun by generous donations from people such as Mahatma Gandhi and Swami Akhandanand. Gandhi also laid the foundation stone in 1933, just before leaving Ahmedabad on his famous Salt March. The building's most distinctive element is its dome, above the entrance. Protruding eaves run along the facade, which is further decorated with various types of grills. Inside, there is a beautiful hall decorated with tile work giving access to the various different wings of the building. The book collection is to the rear. On the right-hand side is a small hall which contains historical maps and images of Ahmedabad.

7 Vadilal Sarabhai Hospital

To continue the walk follow Paldi Road in a southerly direction, cross the junction and after 150 metres you will find the entrance to the Vadilal Sarabhai Hospital on your left-hand side. This historic three-storey hospital was established in 1931 with funds donated by the Sarabhai family. The hospital buildings are another example of Indo-Saracenic architecture, featuring exposed-brick facades and long white eaves extending all along the first floor. The main buildings of the hospital are organized around a small traffic circle. The ward to the right is fitted with a clock tower, while the one on the left is, unfortunately, in bad condition. The hospital was originally planned to have 120 beds but due to increasing demand now has 1,150! Luckily, a new multi-storey hospital is being built just behind the old building, which was recently saved from demolition—the municipality had wanted to create a parking area in its place.

8 Kocharab Ashram

Gandhi Memorial Museum
Opening times: daily, 10am to 6pm (closed Monday)
Admission: free

Head back to the main road and turn left towards the Paldi crossroads. After 250 metres, at the second lane on your left, stands a historic bungalow dating from 1901 hidden away behind the trees. Another 350 metres down Paldi Road stands the Kocharab Ashram. When Mahatma Gandhi came back from South Africa in 1915 he decided to settle in Ahmedabad. Fellow barrister Jinval Desai had come into contact with Gandhi and made his bungalow available for use as Gandhi's first ashram in India. Gandhi called it the Satyagrah Ashram and stayed here for one-and-a-half years before moving to the better-known Gandhi Ashram further north. He found he had to relocate because the plot on which the Satyagrah Ashram stands did not provide enough space for the farming and animal husbandry that Gandhi wanted to do. The building itself is a small whitewashed two-storey bungalow in the British colonial style. There are also some other buildings on the plot housing the kitchen and visitors' hostels. Inside the bungalow is a small **Gandhi Memorial Museum** which has artefacts and photos as well as the list of living rules that Gandhi established in the house.

9 National Institute of Design

Opening times: Monday to Friday, 9am to 6pm
Admission: free
www.nid.edu
+91-79-2662 9500

Head towards the Paldi crossroad and take a left. After 500 metres, just before the start of the bridge take a right to reach the entrance of the National Institute of Design. In the years after Indian independence rapid industrialization brought the need for an institute of industrial design. The government was committed to this and in 1958 invited American architects Charles and Ray Eames to make a tour of India and make recommendations (using a grant from the Ford Foundation). Based on their experience they made a report that would lead to the foundation of the National Institute of Design (NID), and a collaboration was started with the Sarabhai family.

The institute was conceived as an open building where inside and outside spaces would flow together. To that end, the ground floor is largely open, and is well-shaded by the two floors of classrooms above. Light enters via light wells and courtyards open to the sky. Nowadays, lush trees have grown all over the campus so that the pilotis (piers) of the ground floor seamlessly merge with the trees around the building. The building is constructed out of an exposed brick-and-concrete structure. Directly adjacent to it sits a medieval tomb that forms the backdrop of a small amphitheatre.

10 Sanskar Kendra

Ahmedabad City Museum (including the Kite Museum)
Opening times: daily, 10am to 6pm (closed Monday)
Admission: free
+91-79-26578369

Opposite the National Institute of Design stands the Sanskar Kendra which houses the **Ahmedabad City Museum**. Sanskar Kendra is one of the four buildings designed by Le Corbusier in Ahmedabad. While working in Chandigarh in 1951, Le Corbusier was invited by the Ahmedabad municipality to design a museum for them. He used the opportunity to continue developing his ideas about a twentieth-century museum—one of unlimited growth—and arranged so that it could grow organically around a central core. The museum was to be a "contemporary tool for the application and visualization of problems facing modern society". The museum in Ahmedabad, which was finished in 1956, would eventually become one of the three buildings he built using these ideals (the others are in Chandigarh and Tokyo).

Le Corbusier was assisted in his construction by local architect B.V. Doshi and structural engineer Ove Arap (a British national famous for his work on the Sydney Opera House). The distinctly modern style of Le Corbusier can be seen in the design. The reinforced-concrete building stands on a series of pilotis—or columns—and sets up a structural grid of 7 by 7 metres. These bays are replicated seven times in both directions to form a 50-metre square. The entrance is in the building's central courtyard, from which a ramp rises. The rest of the facades are exposed brick. In a way, the building remains unfinished, as can be seen from the drawings on display inside it. Sky bridges from the first level were supposed to connect to three pavilions around the main building, in what would look like a swastika from above. To deal with the intense heat of the summer the roof was designed as a water garden but due to

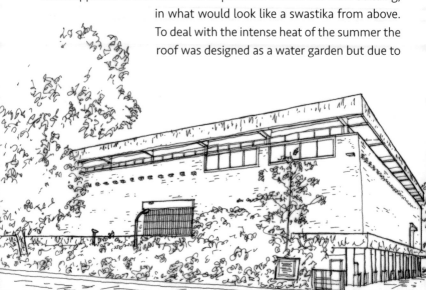

lack of maintenance it began to leak and was abandoned. Similarly, the facades were to be covered by vegetation from the specially designed, curved concrete planters stretching along the bottom of the first floor. The building still functions as a museum and has a permanent exhibition on the history of Ahmedabad. The ground floor also houses a **Kite Museum**, which shows the large variety of kites used during the Uttarayan festival in January of each year.

11 Tagore Memorial Hall

Admission: free

Within the same grounds as the Sanskar Kendra stands the Tagore Memorial Hall. This was built in 1971 as a memorial to the world-renowned Bengali poet Rabindranath Tagore. He is best known for his work *Gitanjali* (written by him originally in Bengali) for which he was awarded the Nobel Prize for Literature in 1913. Tagore's most memorable work, however, might possibly be the national anthems he wrote for both India and Bangladesh.

The exposed-concrete structure was designed by B.V. Doshi in 1966. He received help from the famous structural engineer Mahendra Raj, who conceived the complex folded-plate structural system for the long spans. Mahendra Raj is also known for his qualitative and innovative designs and has not only worked with Doshi but also with many of India's greatest architects, including Correa and Kanvinde. The sculptural reinforced-concrete frames span 33 metres and penetrate the facade setting up a rhythm that can be seen from outside the building. The seating arrangement, which provides space for over 700 people, has an independent structure from that of the exterior walls. The hall is used for a variety of performances and events all year round.

Link to the Jamalpur Walk:
Cross the Sabarmati river via Sardar Patel Bridge.

Jamalpur

Nearest BRTS: Raikhad Char Rasta
Walking time: 2 hours

The area of Jamalpur occupies the southernmost part of the walled city. Jamalpur was one of the original seven *pur*s or neighbourhoods of the city that each housed a Muslim nobleman with his own court. Most of the housing areas are relatively new, compared to the core of the old city in Raipur and Kalupur. Most of the dwellings are also smaller and simpler than the large merchant houses in Raipur. The central feature of this area is the Gaekwad Fort, which was used first by the Marathas and then the British as a base for their control of the city. Behind (north of) the fort are a number of large open spaces, including the riverfront and Victoria Gardens, both of which have acted as public space for the city for a very long time.

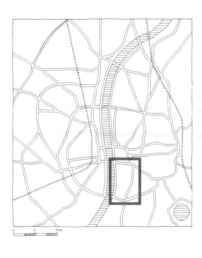

Key

1. Flower Market
2. Baba Lulu Masjid
3. Hebat Khan ki Masjid
4. Khan Jahan Masjid
5. Gaekwad Haveli
6. Tomb of Sardar Khan
7. Khand ni Sheri
8. Diwan's Bungalow
9. Ravivari (Sunday Market)
10. Victoria Gardens

Walk 11

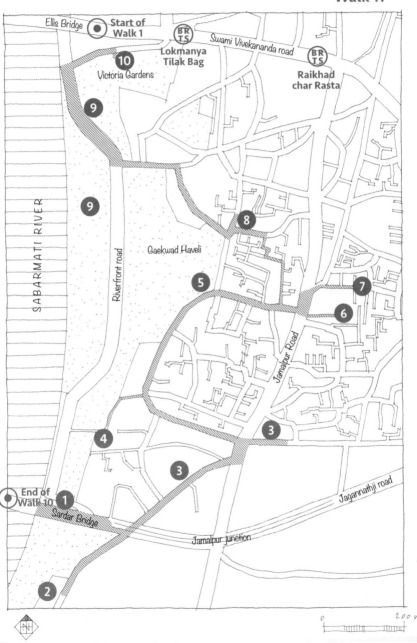

Ellis Bridge   **Start of Walk 1**

BR TS   Swami Vivekananda road

Lokmanya Tilak Bag

BR TS

Raikhad char Rasta

10

Victoria Gardens

9

9

SABARMATI RIVER

Riverfront road

Gaekwad Haveli

8

5

7

6

Jamalpur Road

4

3

3

End of Walk 10

1

Sardar Bridge

Jagannathji road

Jamalpur Junction

2

N

0   200 m

1 Flower Market

Opening times: daily (main market activity between 4–9am)
Admission: free

Just beside Sardar Bridge, across the Sabarmati, lies the Jamalpur flower market. Every day the entire road turns shades of bright yellow, pink and white that together with the fragrances makes for a special experience. The market starts early each morning (around 4am) and much of its business is over by 9am, before the sun gets too strong. Traders and flower workers, however, continue to work during the day.

The market was started in 1989 and has been a hub of the flower business ever since. There is a formal market inside a building at the back, but much of the market spills over onto the street. Flowers have a special significance in India, symbolizing special qualities or gods. The flower garlands are mainly used to decorate idols, especially in the festival season, and also hung over the front doors of houses. Some of the most popular flowers sold here include the Indian rose and marigolds. Apart from flowers it is also possible to buy everything needed for making garlands.

2 Baba Lulu Masjid

Opening times: daily, dawn to dusk (closed during prayers)
Admission: free

The mosque is quietly hidden away, located in an informal settlement opposite the flower market. To find it, continue walking east towards the flyover. Keep this to your left and head into the small lane on your right. This lane has squatter houses on each side and the road itself can be a bit muddy. The mosque can be entered through a small metal gate. The front part of the compound is used as a burial ground. The entrance building is situated slightly higher, behind the graves. To enter the mosque, though, you have to use a side entrance on the left-hand

side. Like most of the medieval mosques in Ahmedabad, the minarets are no longer standing. The beautifully carved bases of them, however, can still be seen. The central dome is slightly elevated, to create the appearance of a small pavilion. Light enters from above, giving the prayer hall a pretty luminescence. There are two *jharoka*s on either side of the mosque; these are better viewed from outside (since the views from them are not terribly interesting).

3 Hebat Khan ki Masjid

Opening times: daily, dawn to dusk (closed during prayers)
Admission: free

From Baba Lulu Masjid, head back along the lane, cross the space underneath the flyover, and turn into the street that leads diagonally away from the main road. After 150 metres it is worthwhile to stop at the **Hathikhana Elephant Grounds** on your left-hand side. Like at the flower market, it helps if you get here early since the elephants are out most of the rest of the day; they return home to the grounds again around dusk. Here they are provided with shelter and food.

Continue along the street until you reach **Jamalpur Darwaza**, one of the original city gates. From here the road would have originally led south to the coast. Jamalpur Darwaza has a typical Ahmedabadi design for city gates, with a single arch, lotus medallions and small protruding decorative cabinets.

Walk towards the city gate and take the road to the right from the gate for about 100 metres. On your left will be the **Hebat Khan ki Masjid**. This simple-looking mosque, unfortunately rigged up with a metal ceiling fan, is actually one of the oldest mosques in Ahmedabad. Its simple style, with two small minarets near the main entrance, dates it to the early fifteenth century. The interior is impressive, with three large richly decorated domes. Material for these was probably looted from nearby Hindu and Jain temples. Another hint to its great age is the small entrance pavilion at the main entrance to the west that looks distinctly Hindu in style. In front of the mosque is a closed-off staircase that led to an underground water tank. Hebat Khan has a tomb in another part of the city.

4 Khan Jahan Masjid

Opening times: daily, dawn to dusk (mosque closed to non-Muslims)
Admission: free (photography prohibited)

From Hebat Khan ki Masjid, walk back to Jamalpur Road and head west. After about 400 metres turn left into a small lane and you will see the Khan Jahan Masjid. This odd-looking edifice is probably one of the strangest juxtapositions of Ahmedabad.

Khan Jahan's original name was Rai Mandlik and he was ruler of the Kingdom of Junagadh in western Gujarat. Mahmud Begada, who ruled Ahmedabad from 1458 to 1511, conquered this kingdom but spared Rai Mandlik's life and even gave him an important position in his new administration. The mosque is built on the very south-western corner of the walled city of Ahmedabad. It is a modest seven-bay structure

JAMALPUR

with small domes crowning each bay. There are two small minarets at opposite ends of the building, although not much of these remain.

The architectural style places the mosque's construction at the early part of the sixteenth century. The **Khan Jahan Darwaza**, next to the mosque, now opens onto a small amphitheatre that is part of the Sabarmati Riverfront Project. The mosque also contains a *madrassa*, or Islamic religious school, with around 300 students. It is the biggest *madrassa* in Ahmedabad and probably for that reason felt it needed to expand further. They chose to build the school partly on top of the old mosque in a style that is more reminiscent of West African adobe buildings than of anything Indian. Nevertheless, it is a striking view, best admired from the amphitheatre outside the city gate. Be careful upon entering the building; the central courtyard is accessible but non-Muslims are not allowed inside the mosque or anywhere else inside the complex. Photography is prohibited in all parts of the complex.

5 Gaekwad Haveli

Upon leaving Khan Jahan Masjid, head north for around 350 metres. Soon, you will be walking alongside the fortification of the Gaekwad Haveli (also known as Gaekwad Fort), one of the few buildings built in the city under Maratha rule.

The end of the seventeenth century saw continuous warfare between the Mughal Empire to the north and the Marathas to the south. In this period Ahmedabad was attacked by Maratha forces a number of times. The city was looted in 1708, and an invading army was bought off in 1725. Then, finally, in 1738 the Mughals and Marathas agreed to a joint jurisdiction of the city. The *haveli* served as a residence for the new Maratha administrators. It is named after Damaji Gaekwad, the man who negotiated the treaty. In 1753 the city found itself exclusively under Maratha rule when an armed force expelled the Mughals; they were gone forever.

Possession of the *haveli* changed hands again when the city came under British rule in 1818. It served as cantonment and also functioned as a warehouse for the railways. The fort currently houses the Ahmedabad Crime Branch. The tower just inside the entry gate is accessible to the public. This tower, built in 1738, is intended to be home to a new police museum dedicated to highlighting the role this service played during the communal struggles in the city.

6 Tomb of Sardar Khan

Follow the street opposite the Gaekwad Haveli for 200 metres, keeping your eyes open because it is full of interesting old *havelis*, and you will come to a set of stairs leading down to the Jamalpur Road and the entrance to the Tomb of Sardar Khan. This tomb, built in 1685, is hidden among the dense city fabric and is one of the few Islamic monuments built during Mughal rule. The complex is entered via a crumbling Hindu-style gate, one that has only one of its *chhatri*s still standing (on the left-hand corner). Nawab Sardar Khan was Minister of

Ahmedabad during the reign of Emperor Aurangzeb. This brick tomb lies to the rear of the plot and has to be approached via an informal settlement that has formed itself in what used to be its open court.

The plan of the tomb is formed by two concentric squares; the outer one consists of twenty pillars enclosing a veranda, while the inner one has twelve pillars surrounding the tomb. The magnificent

onion-shaped domes on the roof contrast starkly in style with the Indo-Saracenic style of the base of the tomb and indicate Sardar Khan's Persian origins. His name is remembered because of his crucial involvement in the struggle for the Mughal throne that took place between brothers Aurangzeb and Dara after Emperor Shah Jahan suffered a stroke in 1657. Dara was the preferred successor and initially gained the upper hand but was defeated in battle by Aurangzeb. Dara then fled to Lahore and onto Ajmer where he tried to organize an army. Sardar Khan offered support to Dara but betrayed him and Dara was beaten in battle and paraded around on an elephant in Delhi before being executed in 1659.

7 Khand ni Sheri

Head back to Jamalpur Road and take a right. Take another right at the first opportunity and head inside the small lane on your right. Khand ni Sheri is one of the best preserved clusters of *pol* houses. This *pol* is essentially T-shaped, which is the direct result of the introduction of municipal sewers, which—being made of terracotta—could be laid in straight lines only.

The *haveli*s at the back of Khand ni Sheri are the most prominent. Two storeys high with a pitched roof, brackets shaped like elephant trunks support the second floor, which is also decoratively carved with floral motifs. The house next to it is painted shades of blue and has a slightly higher *otla* but is otherwise quite similar in proportion. In a working class *pol* such as this one, it is still possible to observe some building traditions that are not present in the wealthy merchant houses. Many houses still have steep ladder-like stairs and use clay storage jars. Originally, the houses would have been similar to village dwellings, using mud and thatch for the walls and *lipan* (cow-dung mixed with mud plaster) on the floors inside the house. It is only over time that the *kachcha* houses turned into *pakka* houses (very similar to contemporary processes in informal settlements).

⑧ Diwan's Bungalow

Opening times: daily, 7am to 11pm
Admission: free
Divansbungalow@neemranahotels.com
+91-79-25355428

To reach Diwan's bungalow head back to the entrance of Sardar Khan Tomb and head up the stairs. Take the first lane right and follow the *pol* till it emerges on the main road. Take a right and you will find the bungalow overlooking the junction. This two storey whitewashed building is the ancestral home of the Kadri family who can trace their lineage back to the city of Baghdad. The man who commissioned this house in the middle of the nineteenth century was the Diwan or Government Minister of the Princely State of Radhanpur. After the decline of the Mughal Empire most parts of Gujarat came under Maratha rule but Radhanpur established itself as an independent kingdom in 1753. This later became a British protectorate, which

explains why there was a Diwan living in Ahmedabad from 1813 onwards. The architect is believed to be an Englishman, which seems plausible looking at the highly decorative Corinthian capitals and gothic window frames. The most notable feature of the building's exterior, however, is the huge protruding wooden *jharoka*, clearly inspired by local influences. The building is now part of the Neemrana Hotels chain, which manages heritage hotels across India. The door immediately below the *jharoka* leads to the reception and breakfast room, and these can be accessed during the hotel's normal opening hours. There are eight rooms in the hotel.

9 Ravivari (Sunday Market)

Opening times: Sundays, dawn to dusk
Admission: free

From the Diwan's Bungalow retrace your steps for about 50 metres and turn to the right. The road will gently curve to the right for around 250 metres before ending up at a T-junction. Take a left and head towards the old gate you will see in front of you. Behind this gate lies the riverbank, which has long been used as a market, and has been so since the very foundation of the city in the fifteenth century. This lively market offers everything from clothing and kitchen utensils to animals, books, furniture and tools, not to mention food and drink. It used to be set up on the seasonally dry riverbed, but as part of the Sabarmati River Regeneration Project has recently been resettled to its current position on a new concrete embankment. For an idea of what it used to be like, take a look at the photos mounted on the side of the toilet blocks and you will see the different incarnations of the market over time. Currently it consists of around 1,200 individual vendors and the best time to visit is early in the morning because of the midday heat, but the market is open all day.

⑩ Victoria Gardens

Opening times: daily, dawn to dusk
Admission: free

When leaving the riverbank keep an eye out for a remarkable two-storey **Mahalaxmi temple** on your right. This Hindu temple was constructed in a European neoclassical style, which is very unusual. This symmetrical building shows only a few Hindu decorative elements. Most notable of these is the Krishna figure in the small tympanum at the top of the building, recognizable by the flute in his hands. Sometimes there is an elephant standing in front of the temple, with a mahout taking money and offerings from devotees. Continue walking away from the river and you will come to the **Victoria Gardens** on your right. These gardens were built by the British and are estimated to be around two-hundred years old. A statue of Queen Victoria graces the central portion; somewhat neglected in recent years, it is now in very bad condition. Fortunately, however, there are plans to give the park a facelift, and connect it to the nearby riverfront.

End of walks.

Further Afield

This chapter covers sites and monuments that are a little outside the city ambit, or do not fall conveniently into any of the city walks. Except for the twentieth-century Sangath, all monuments are from the early history of the city, a time when many saints and noblemen decided to settle in close proximity to one another around the city. Sarkhej Roza and Shah-e-Alam Roza are both large complexes with several important buildings. The Adalaj stepwell and Dada Hari stepwell are two of the best examples of the stepwell typology, a characteristic of this region, as almost all important buildings had water as a central feature.

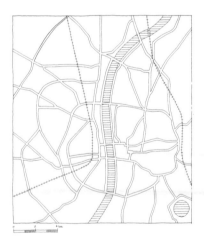

Key

1. Kankaria Lake
2. Sangath
3. Shah-e-Alam Roza
4. Sarkhej Roza
5. Dada Hari Vav
6. Adalaj Vav

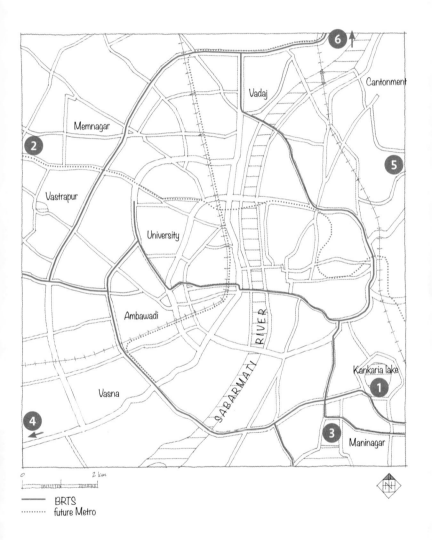

BRTS
.... future Metro

1 Kankaria Lake

Opening times: daily, 9am to 6pm
Admission charges

Ahmedabad zoo (Kamla Nehru Zoological Garden)
Opening times: daily, 9am to 5.30pm
Admission charges

The easiest way to reach Kankaria Lake is by BRTS, in which case you will enter via Gate 1 on the western side. It is also possible to walk from Raipur Gate, which is approximately one kilometre to the southwest of the Gate 3 entrance. Hauz-e-Qutb, better known as Kankaria Lake, is a man-made water tank constructed during the reign of Qutbuddin Ahmed Shah, grandson of the founder of Ahmedabad, Ahmed Shah I. Qutbuddin ruled Ahmedabad for only seven years from 1451 and yet he managed to have this enormous 600-metre-wide (2,000-foot) tank built. The tank collects water during the monsoon and can then be used as a water source throughout the rest of the year. The fact that such a tank was necessary is a testimony to the growth and success of Ahmedabad in the early decades after its foundation in 1414. There are steps all around the entire water body, as well as small temple-like pavilions.

The lake was entirely redeveloped in 2008, when all kinds of attractions were added to this historic precinct. The central feature of the lake is the artificial island at its heart, with a causeway aligned precisely due south. The island is called Nagina Wadi, meaning 'beautiful garden' in Urdu. The eastern side of the lake, at Gate 4, has the inlet sluice. This massive sandstone structure was used to control the lake's water level and to ensure no debris entered it. The inlet into the lake is also carved like the buttresses of mosque minarets, although you really have to be in a boat to fully appreciate them.

The northern edge of the lake is where the **Ahmedabad zoo** (official name **Kamla Nehru Zoological Garden**) is located, which can be entered from the lake side. The zoo was established in 1951 by Reuben David, an Ahmedabad-born Jew who had trained himself to be a veterinarian. The zoo has various indigenous species from across India, including lions, tigers, crocodiles and black buck deer. There are also the more common langurs, bats and elephants, which are native to Ahmedabad (which begs the question why they have to be locked up in cages?) The western side of the lake contains the One Tree Hill Park, which contains **Dutch Tombs**. This cluster of tombs features the final resting place of both Dutch and English merchants, as well as some Armenians. During the seventeenth century both the Dutch and English had set up factories (trading posts) in north-western India, processing goods like cotton and indigo. Most of these factories were located in Surat, which is much closer to the sea, but some were established here. There are four main graves, three of them built in the fashion of Mughal tombs, and one with a pyramid-shaped gravestone.

2 Sangath

Opening times: garden open on weekdays, 10am to 6pm
(studio open between 1.30 and 2pm)
Admission: free (groups need prior appointment)
www.sangath.org
+91-79-27454537

Located on the busy Drive-in Road, Sangath is the architectural office founded and conceived by India's one of the most important architects, Balkrishna Doshi. A key figure in post-Independence India's architectural profession together with other architects like Charles Correa and Kanvinde, Doshi was able to give modern Indian architecture a distinct identity by carefully moulding context and culture, tradition and technology. Sangath is an excellent example of this tradition as it offers a wealth of references to ancient and contemporary architecture which Doshi has managed to seamlessly blend together. It is possible to recognize elements from ancient Jain temples, the architecture studio of Le Corbusier, traditional

dwellings and ancient Hindu symbolism. Doshi started his training as an architect in the Sir J.J. College of Art in Mumbai, which was at that time headed by Claude Bartley, who had designed several buildings in Ahmedabad. Doshi soon decided to move to Europe where he came into contact with Le Corbusier, who had just been commissioned to design the city of Chandigarh as the new state capital of Punjab. Doshi worked in Paris for four years and eventually managed the projects of Le Corbusier in India. It was then that he decided to start his own office in Ahmedabad.

He was initially working out of a building in the old city, close to Bhadra, when he started construction of his own studio in 1979. The office that Doshi founded is called Vastu Shilpa, meaning 'design of environment', and his new studio became emblematic of that ideal. Doshi bought a plot of land when it was still outside the city and it was in this rural setting that he decided to place the building in the north-east corner so that the rest of the site could be left open as a garden. The forecourt gives a glimpse into his studio, but Doshi deliberately designed it so that in order to enter you must walk through the garden. Along this route you will see a stone mosaic reminiscent of the *jaali* on the Sidi Saiyed Masjid; this commemorates the mango tree that used to stand there. Further on, beside the Indian lotus pond, you will find the best place to see the overall structure of the building. The main studio is essentially subterranean to protect it from the summer heat. This allows the garden to naturally blend with the steps of the amphitheatre and the roof. To further counter the heat, sunlight comes in either from the north, as in the main studio, or reflected via light wells. The roof covered is in china mosaic tiles that reflect the sunlight and are recycled from waste material like the paving. In the monsoon, water cascades down the roof along a system of basins to the pond at the far end of the garden. Because the studio is subterranean you enter it by going underneath the vault farthest to the left. The interior of the building is divided into two parts. The one on the left contains a foundation along with conference rooms, while the main architectural studio is on the right. As befitting an architectural practice, the walls and ceilings are covered with numerous models of all Vastu Shilpa's projects designed over the years. Doshi decided to name the building Sangath, meaning 'moving together through participation', which has served the office well until now. The garden and reception area are open to visitors during office hours and it is possible to be shown around the building at lunchtime (1.30pm on weekdays) without prior appointment.

Close by, along Drive-in Road, stands another building by Doshi, the **Gandhi Labour Institute**. The institute was established in 1979 to provide a study and education around the themes of employment, industry and social justice. Architecturally, the institute looks like Sangath's big brother. Like Sangath, the building itself constitutes a small mound, topped by a series of vaulted roofs. Steps lead you up to the main entrance that gives way to a large central hall that connects all the various rooms. One side of the central hall opens up to a small courtyard, while the other side opens up to a garden with amphitheatre. Hostels and various supporting functions snake along the edge of this garden and give it an informal edge.

3 Shah-e-Alam Roza

Opening times: daily, dawn to dusk.
Admission: free

This Roza lies about 3 kilometres (1.85 miles) south of the walled city and is most easily reached by auto rickshaw or by BRTS (alight at the Mira Cinema crossroads station). Shah-e-Alam literally means 'king of the world', but this was only ever a nominal title, as Sayyid Muhammad was a Muslim religious teacher and never ruled the city of Ahmedabad. Although he never ruled the city, he did marry into the royal family and played an important role in the social and political environment of the city. He arrived during the rule of Ahmed Shah I and settled on the outskirts of the city. He paid regular visits to the Sufi saint Ganj Baksh, who had settled at Sarkhej Roza. As a teacher, he taught the sons of one of the most celebrated rulers of Ahmedabad, Mahmud Begada. It was noblemen at his court that initiated and financed the construction of the complex as we see it today.

When Shah-e-Alam died in 1475, construction began on his tomb, which was completed eight years later in 1483. The tomb has the typical pattern of an outer wall with *jaali*s that surround the central enclosure which contains the actual grave. The aisle in-between the outer wall and the inner enclosure is roofed by smaller domes, while the tomb chamber has a larger dome. The floor is of marble, as are some parts of the inner enclosure. There is a small tomb right next to the main tomb that contains, among other remains, a parrot, a pet of Shah-e-Alam; he was so fond of the bird that it was buried with him. The construction of the seven-bay mosque might have started as early as the sixteenth century, but was only finished around 1620. Its style is an example of late Sultanate architecture, with an open facade and minarets at opposite ends of the front facade. Another tomb to the south and similar in style and layout is of one of Shah-e-Alam's descendants. In addition to the mosque and tombs, the complex had a number of entrance gates similar in style to the city gates of Ahmedabad. A large water tank to the south of the complex has been encroached upon by a large informal settlement.

4 Sarkhej Roza

Opening times: daily, dawn to dusk.
Admission: free

The complex of Sarkhej Roza, located about 7 kilometres (4.35 miles) to the southwest of the city centre, was built over a period of decades from 1445 onwards. There is no convenient public-transport access, so the easiest way to reach it is by rickshaw or private transport. Expect to travel twenty-five minutes from the city centre in Paldi. The central feature of this complex is a large water tank measuring 200 by 240 metres around which several palaces, tombs and mosque have been constructed. When the famous Modernist architect Le Corbusier came here in the 1950s he correctly called it the "acropolis of Ahmedabad".

The best place to start your exploration of this fascinating complex is the main cluster of buildings north of the water tank. After removing your shoes, you will enter a large courtyard around which three buildings are ranged. The **Tomb of Ganj Baksh** is positioned on your right, with royal tombs on the left and a mosque to the rear. Ganj Baksh, meaning 'bestower of treasures', was a Sufi saint born in the early fourteenth century. He had made a pilgrimage to Mecca in 1388 and after returning to India was witness to the devastation of Timur's army. He moved to the capital of Gujarat at Patan, where he decided to settle down permanently. Before Ahmedabad had even been founded, Ganj decided to settle at Sarkhej, a prospering village of weavers and indigo dyers. In turn, the saint convinced Ahmed Shah to found the new capital at the banks of the nearby Sabarmati river. When Ganj Baksh died in 1445, Ahmed Shah built a tomb for him, one that was finally finished in 1451. The white-washed tomb is double height, with stone *jaali*s all across the top of the facade. It measures 32 metres square and consists of 13 bays, out of which four form the central chamber holding the grave. The grave itself is delicately carved marble. Directly to the west of the tomb stands the **mosque** that was erected at the same time. Its overall layout, with an arcade around its courtyard and a women's prayer area at mezzanine level, are similar to the Jama Masjid, as is the simple detailing of the columns. The prayer hall, however, is less than impressive, as it lacks the grand facade with minarets and elevated ceilings of the Jama Masjid. A wide porch

protrudes from the south side of the mosque with several *jaroka*s that offer lovely views of the lake.

The third building in the compound is the **Tomb of Mahmud Begada**, which is also where his queen and sons are buried. The tomb of the queen is closest to the mosque, and because it is located on the corner it offers wonderful views of the lake. Part of the tomb displays information panels about the whole complex. Both of the tombs here have successive squares of pillars, with the outer ones boasting of beautifully carved *jaali*s.

Mahmud Begada added to the complex by constructing the lake and summer palaces on the south-eastern embankment. The smaller of these is the **King's Palace**, which contains a gateway from the bed of the lake to outside the compound. The top floor is columned hall and has several simple *jharoka*s. The **Queen's Palace** is slightly larger and more graceful. From the lakeside the palace appears to have two floors, but the lower one is actually only a passageway in front of the earthen embankment. The colonnades of the facade extend across both floors, and instead of having *jharoka*s, like on the King's Palace, these protrude in two places to form porches. Staircases lead you up from the lower level. Behind the palace stand the tombs of a number of Siddi noblemen; these were added only at the end of the sixteenth century. The noblemen, originally of African descent, probably ruled parts of this region in the chaotic period between the Battle of Diu in 1537 and the annexation of the Sultanate by the Mughals in 1573. Finally, there is the **sluice gate** at the northern edge of the tank which

connects a secondary body of water to the main lake and is large enough to walk through. Its mouth is marked by carvings that look like the bastions of a minaret.

5 Dada Hari Vav

Opening times: daily, dawn to dusk
Admission: free

Although less decorative than its bigger brother at Adalaj (see below), the Dada Hari Vav, or stepwell, is still a majestic piece of architecture, and well worth a visit. The well is located around one kilometre (0.6 miles) outside the walled city and is easily reachable by auto rickshaw. It was constructed in 1500, just one year after the well in Adalaj. It was commissioned by Dada Hari (also known as Bai Harir) who was superintendent of the Sultan Mahmud Begada's harem. Like other high-placed noblemen at court, he had enough funds to build his own mosque and tomb. Unlike some other noblemen, though, he decided to also include a stepwell. The well provided water for the large garden attached to the compound, which would also explain why the complex was located just outside the city walls. The remains of the mechanism by which water was provided to the mosque, and possibly the garden, is still visible at the top of the well. In fact, there are essentially two wells, one that is circular goes deep, and one that is octagonal has a more ceremonial function. The ceremonial well is reached by descending five storeys from the entrance-level pavilion. Parts of it are open-air and others closed, letting in light while supporting the ground around it. The carving is simple and features trees, lotuses and other floral motifs. The mosque at the back of the complex is built out of sandstone and is in the style of the early Sultanate, with a pair of minarets flanking the entrance. The front facade is an amalgamation of arches and other openings, including two *jharoka*s. The tomb is similar to that of Rani Sipri but lacks the stone screens on the outer veranda. It is possible to access the roof of the mosque via a staircase inside the buttress of the minaret.

6 **Adalaj Vav**

Opening times: daily, 6am to 6 pm
Admission: free

This stepwell (or *vav*) is located in Adalaj village, which is about 18 kilometres (11 miles) north of Ahmedabad. It is best to arrange your own transport for a return journey by hiring a taxi or auto rickshaw. Expect to pay around Rs 400-500 for a return journey—make sure you ask the driver to wait. Of all the stepwells in this area, the Adalaj Vav is probably the most impressive, mainly because of its size, the quality of its carving, and its excellent state of preservation. Almost completely intact, it probably has the same overwhelming impression on visitors as it did 600 years ago when it was built by Mahmud Begada, ruler of Ahmedabad from 1458 to 1511. Construction was started, however, by Rana Veer Singh, the ruler of a Hindu kingdom conquered by Mahmud Begada in 1498. He killed Rana Veer Singh and the legend goes that in order for Mahmud to marry Rana's widow he had to promise her to finish the stepwell. After Mahmud had done so he came for his prize but the queen, wanting to remain loyal to her late husband, committed suicide by jumping into the well instead.

The stepwell is organized in a series of five levels, which slowly descend towards the water. As you go down you will notice the temperature dropping. Each level—each step even—gives you a slightly different vista as the columns, beams and floors sequentially open and close to allow in light at different points. The stepwell looks like a cross in plan, with one elongated axis that leads to the well itself and three shorter arms that serve as the entrances, and it is hard to miss out on the unique arrangement of these axes. The stepwell is constructed from sandstone in a trabeated way, meaning that all distances are spanned using interconnected horizontal beams. The entrance has several *jharoka*s, similar in style to the ones later used in mosques in Ahmedabad. The intricate carving features many floral patterns, as well as elephants. The stepwell actually contains two separate wells. The processional staircase connecting to the first well is octagonal in plan and decoratively carved. This well connects to a circular one at the back that has no decoration and is purely functional. There are two spiral staircases, one on each side of the well, that directly connect to the ground level. In a semi-desert climate like that of Gujarat and Rajasthan, water is a highly prized commodity. This stepwell forms part of a strong tradition of building wells and other water-collecting devices. There are more than 120 stepwells in Gujarat alone. These buildings were not only utilitarian but also acted as symbolic places that showed the might of the ruler by the size of the well and quality of the carvings. (Other famous stepwells include Rani ki Vav in Patan and Chand Baoli, in-between Jaipur and Agra.)

Architectural Styles

This chapter explains some of the architectural styles mentioned in the book. These are mentioned in loose chronological order, starting from the oldest and ending with the most recent.

Nagara/Solanki

Nagara-style temple architecture is one of the main groups in which temples in India can be classified (others include Dravidian and Kalinga). Any Nagara-style temple is made up of a series of squares, hierarchically and symmetrically organized, connecting the inner sanctum with the main entrance. People enter via an entrance pavilion or *ardha mandapa* that connects with the inner sanctum or *garbha griha* where the deity resides. Above the deity is the towering structure of the *shikhara*. Sometimes, there is an additional vestibule or *antarala* in-between these spaces. The main construction material is always stone used in a trabeated manner, meaning that a system of posts and lintels are used as opposed to arches. Many regional variants exist but they all follow the same basic structure, differing only in their architectural details, such as carvings. In Gujarat, the Solanki style is dominant, and it is most easily recognizable by the use of *torana*s, or decorative serpentine arches.

Jain

Stylistically the architecture of Jain temples is not unlike those found in Hindu temples. The mutual coexistence of Jainism and Hinduism in India means they share many features, for example, temple layout and carved motifs. Most Jain temples have a *garbha griha* and a pillared *mandapa*. The form and layout of Jain temples can vary enormously; there is not a single dominant typology. Temples built outside of the old city have a ceremonial compound wall built on a high plinth (or *jagati*). Even temples in the old city of Ahmedabad always sit on a small plinth but tend to be more compact in form—these sometimes also include a sacred subterranean part. Jain temples are often completely constructed of white marble, and another characteristic feature is the prolific use of *torana*s.

Sultanate

The Sultanate style of architecture represents a blend of Indian and Iranian (originally known as Persian) elements. Muslim sultans had conquered parts of northern India from the twelfth century onwards and they commissioned new buildings. It was a style primarily used for the construction of mosques, tombs and palaces, often designed by Muslim master-builders but constructed using local Indian craftsmen. The domes and arches often seen in Iranian architecture became prolific elements, as well as the increased use of brick. Experienced Indian stonemasons were able to add carvings in exquisite depth and detail. Other Indian elements, such as *jharoka*s and chhajjas were also introduced as stylistic elements. Representations of figure and deities were not allowed in Muslim architecture so instead floral and geometric motifs became dominant. Many regional variants exist, each adopting local elements and it is possible to recognize Gujarati Sultanate architecture by its coloured sandstone and the extensive use of stone *jaali*s.

Mughal

This architectural style is especially associated with the reign of the Mughals from the sixteenth to the eighteenth centuries. In a way, it is a more developed version of the earlier Sultanate style, and was, again, predominantly used for the construction of tombs—the most famous example would be the Taj Mahal. Compared to the earlier Sultanate style, the Mughal tends to be more bulky; certainly it seems less delicate, relying more on scale and grandeur than on sculptural elements such as carving. The facades are almost exclusively a combination of white marble and red sandstone, and the decorative elements tend to come in the form of inlaid marble making frames and repeating motifs. Mughal buildings are often integrated with their lush gardens and have a classic *char-bagh* layout.

Haveli architecture

The *haveli*s, or traditional townhouses of Ahmedabad, all use a delicate architectural language. A linear platform or *otla* allows interaction between the street and the house. A central courtyard forms the focus of social life in the house and allows light to enter. The *haveli*s in Ahmedabad are organized in *pol*s that are compact gated communities inhabited by a single caste, usually consisting of 40-70 households. The *haveli*s were built of wood by local craftsmen. The wealth of the owner would be reflected in the amount and detail of the wood-carved panels and brackets, which feature human figures, animals and floral motifs. The vernacular style was not only used for

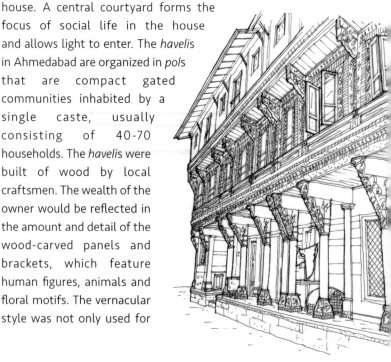

such residential buildings but also sometimes for temples and religious schools.

Neoclassical

Classical architecture flowered in Ancient Greece and Rome in the centuries before and after the birth of Christ. As a style, it was elegant and harmonious, but it disappeared with the fall of the Roman Empire. Neoclassicism was a revival of this in the sixteenth century, first in Italy and then throughout the rest of Europe and North America. It happened largely thanks to Andrea Palladio, an Italian architect who studied the ruins of ancient Rome and adapted their styles to suit his era. With the spread of European empires, the style became global. Neoclassicism was popular in British India for government buildings, as it was in most of the British colonies right up until the outbreak of World War II. Its popularity was probably because these buildings gave the appearance of stability and solidity, plus it was Britain's way of signalling to the world that she was the natural successor to Ancient Rome's great empire.

Gothic

This architectural style was common in Europe, particularly Northern Europe, in the twelfth to sixteenth centuries. Its main characteristics were the pointed arch and the buttress. The gothic style experienced a revival from the middle of the eighteenth century onwards, partly as a reaction to centuries of neoclassicism—a style that was more restrained, even dull—but mainly thanks to the huge popularity of gothic novels. The revival of gothic architecture also used elements from medieval castles such as merlons, meant to evoke a sense of history.

Indo-Saracenic

This style aimed at mixing various elements from the Hindu, Mughal and British architectural traditions. After the establishment of the

British Raj, British architects started adopting Indian architectural elements in all parts of British Empire (including Malaysia and in England itself). The layout of the buildings was most often imported from the West, as were the new functions, but their outer appearances were transformed. The style was used for palaces and also for many new civic buildings like hotels, train stations and courthouses.

Art Deco

This was a style hugely popular internationally in the 1920s and '30s. It takes its name from an exhibition held in Paris in 1925 and is considered to have been the last total design movement, in that its principles could be applied to anything from a cigarette case to an ocean liner. Its lines were simple, sleek and elegant, with lots of emphasis on horizontal planes punctuated with soaring vertical elements such as towers and flagpoles. Initially black, white and chrome were the colours of choice but when translated to the tropics art deco took on softer pastel shades, more in keeping with the climate and the light.

Modern

Modernism describes a wide range of architectural styles that developed in the twentieth century. With the development of reinforced concrete and other technological advances, architects, first in the West then later elsewhere, were able to make a completely new architectural language. What was valued most in this new architecture was clarity of form, with everything completely stripped of traditional motifs, statues or other decorations. The form of the building derived from its function and its materials were exposed as honestly as possible. One of the key figures in the Modern movement was the Swiss-born architect Le Corbusier. His ideas and designs had great influence on architects around the globe, and some of the buildings in Ahmedabad played an important role in this. Another key figure was the American Louis Kahn. The Modern style of Le Corbusier and Kahn gained widespread popularity in India. The term Postmodern is usually applied to the local cultural and climate adaptations of the initial principles of Modern architecture.

Glossary

agiyari: place of worship for Parsis, also known as a Fire Temple

arcade: long arched gallery or veranda, often open at only one side, formed by a series of arches supported by columns or piers

arch: curved structure over opening

Art Deco: style in art and architecture popular in the 1920s and '30s that drew inspiration from industrial elements

buttress: projecting wall support

burj: tower in Arabic

char-rasta: Hindi word for a crossroads

chabutra: ornamental bird-feeder, usually a few metres high and sitting on a pedestal

chhajja: projecting or overhanging roof to provide shade

chhatri: pavilion with domed roof, usually marking corners or other special parts of a building

chowk: square or plaza, often at the heart of a village or neighbourhood

colonnade: row of columns (similar to an arcade)

column: supporting element, always round in shape

dargah: shrine associated with the grave or tomb of a Muslim saint or important political figure

darwaza: large gateway

derasar: Jain temple

dharmashala: guesthouse for travellers usually connected to a temple or religious institution

ghats: series a steps leading down to a body of water

garbha griha: inner sanctum of a Hindu temple containing an idol of the deity

gopuram: colourful and elaborately decorative structure over Hindu temple entrances; usually featuring statues from the Hindu pantheon

Gothic: style of architecture in Western Europe from the twelfth to the sixteenth century; its main features were pointed arches, buttresses and delicately carved stonework.

Haji: male Muslim who has made the pilgrimage to Mecca

haveli: traditional townhouse centered around internal courtyard

GLOSSARY

Hijri calendar: lunar calendar consisting of 354 (or 355) days; the first year of which started in 622 A.D. when Muhammed left Mecca for Medina

Indian National Calendar: Sometimes called the Saka calendar, it is the official civil calendar in use in India, at times also by the Indian government, along with the Gregorian calendar. It started in 78 A.D.

Indo-Saracenic: style mixing elements from Hindu, Mughal and British architecture

jaali: detailed decoration in wood, metal, stone, etc., with regular patterns of openings or holes

jharoka: overhanging enclosed balcony often overlooking a street

Jain: Indian religion which began in the sixth century B.C. and advocated complete asceticism and non-violence

Jain style: Jain temples can vary enormously in form and layout but are often quite similar to Hindu places of worship in their carvings and the fact that they often sit within a ceremonial compound

jhoola: Hindi word for the traditional swing, suspended from the ceiling; called *hinchko* in Gujarati

Khan: A title given to rulers and officials in central and (now) south Asia

kunva: Hindi word for a well

maidan: A large gathering place, usually at the centre of the town, originally a Persian planning concept

mandapa: pillared hall or pavilion used for a variety of religious activities and a common feature in most Hindu temples

mandir: Hindi word for temple

masjid: mosque; a place of worship for followers of Islam which always includes a prayer hall, a *minbar*, *mihrab* and ablution pond

merlon: solid upright section of a battlement parapet

minaret: tall slim tower attached to a mosque from which the muezzin calls the faithful to prayer

mihrab: niche in the *qibla* wall indicating the direction for prayer

minbar: the pulpit from which the Muslim Imam directs prayer

Mughal style: bulky and impressive style associated with the Mughals who ruled India from the sixteenth to the eighteenth century, invariably with inlaid marble and often featuring lush gardens

motif: design element which is repeated

muezzin: person who calls the Muslim faithful to prayer

Nandi: Shiva's mount, a bull, often placed as a guard in front of Shaivite temples

Nagara: consists of a series of squares organised in a hierarchical and symmetrical way, this is one of the main classifications of Indian temples (the others are Dravidian and Kalinga) and the main one found in Gujarat.

Neoclassical: style of architecture popular from the seventeenth century onwards and based on the architecture of ancient Greece and Rome; buildings are usually symmetrical, have elegant proportioning and are characterised by the generous use of columns and pillars.

otla: small raised platform or plinth

pol: literally meaning 'gate' in Gujarati; a traditional housing cluster shared by a single community based on caste or profession

pilaster: an ornamental addition giving the appearance of a supporting column

pur: neighbourhood

roza: Urdu word for a garden complex

shikhara: a towering structure common in most Hindu temples located directly above the deity; literally means 'mountain peak'

Shah: Persian word for king or ruler

Solanki: see Nagara

torana: decorative arch placed as a gateway or surrounding a deity

trabeate: structural system that consists of columns and beams

qibla: direction towards Mecca found in Muslim mosques

vav: Gujarati word for stepwell

Vikram Samvat: a Hindu calendar used in some Indian states and Nepal. It started in 57 B.C.

Index

Acknowledgements

This book could not have been possible without the kind people of Ahmedabad. Matthijs would like to thank all the countless numbers of them who shared their stories, let him into their homes and offered water and tea along the journey. Both of us are also indebted to all writers and researchers that have been documenting Ahmedabad's history and architecture, thus allowing us to compile the book. The idea for this book originated during Matthijs's time at Sangath and he would like to thank B.V. Doshi and all the wonderful people working there for their support. A special thanks goes out to those who volunteered to help him in the fieldwork, translating and offering suggestions, Bidoura Mosharraf, Namrata Deol, Saeb Ali Khan and Freyaan Anklesaria. Matthijs would also like to thank his family and friends for their support, even sometimes from a distance. And finally, both Gregory and Matthijs are grateful for the encouragement from Bipin Shah and all the other people at Mapin without whom the book could not have been made.

Notes

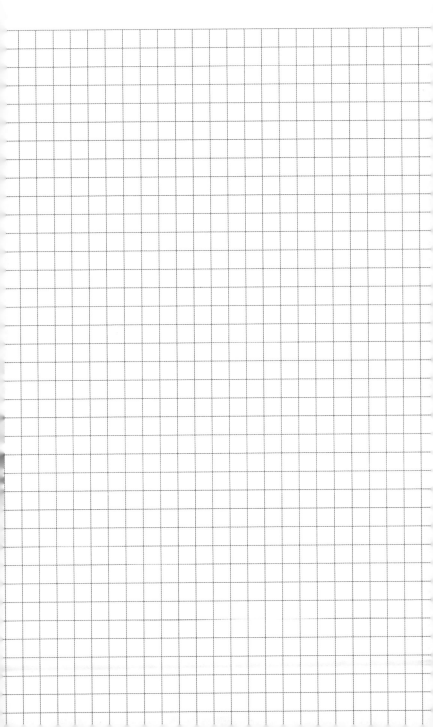